Hot Pot Cookbook for Beginners

HOT POT
COOKBOOK
for Beginners

Flavorful One-Pot Meals
from Korea, China, Thailand,
Mongolia, and More

SUSAN NG

Photography by Elysa Weitala

ROCKRIDGE
PRESS

This book is dedicated to my late father-in-law, Chau Vuong.

To your legacy . . .
in remembering healthy and happy times with
many family hot-pot meals shared together.

For general information on our other products and services or to obtain technical support, please contact our Customer Care Department within the United States at (866) 744-2665, or outside the United States at (510) 253-0500.

Rockridge Press publishes its books in a variety of electronic and print formats. Some content that appears in print may not be available in electronic books, and vice versa.

TRADEMARKS: Rockridge Press and the Rockridge Press logo are trademarks or registered trademarks of Callisto Media Inc. and/or its affiliates, in the United States and other countries, and may not be used without written permission. All other trademarks are the property of their respective owners. Rockridge Press is not associated with any product or vendor mentioned in this book.

Interior and Cover Designer: Francesca Pacchini
Art Producer: Sara Feinstein
Editor: Anne Lowrey
Production Editors: Emily Sheehan and Ruth Sakata Corley
Production Manager: Martin Worthington

Photography © 2021 Elysa Weitala. Food styling by Victoria Woollard. Illustration used under license from Shutterstock.com. Author photo courtesy of Huong Bui.

Paperback ISBN: 978-1-63807-023-8
eBook ISBN: 978-1-63807-814-2
R0

Contents

Introduction

Hi, everyone, my name is Susan. I am a chef and passionate culinary instructor teaching Asian cuisines in Toronto. I grew up enjoying Chinese hot pot, and to me it is the ultimate comfort food. My most memorable childhood dinners were when the family gathered around the table (as soon as it got cold out) to feast on a variety of meat and vegetables simmering flavorfully together in a hot pot. The heaping platters of food, the noise of utensils clinking, the constant chatter, the aromas, and flavors—these meals always ended with a satisfied full belly and were precious moments of family bonding. My early foray into other hot-pot styles were during my travels visiting family: sukiyaki in Japan and *lẩu* hot pot in Vietnam. I just love how each Asian cuisine has its own unique flavors that tantalize the senses in the universal setting of hot pot.

Local hot-pot restaurants were my go-to special-occasion meals with friends, and the best part was trying a bit of everything offered. A rolling hot pot often replaced a roasted turkey as the table's centerpiece in traditional holiday celebrations with my entire family. Today, a hot pot is a regular dinner-time feature with my three children and husband, cooking a combination of Asian pantry items with fresh and leftover ingredients we have in our refrigerator and freezer. Whether you are a novice navigating how to prepare hot pot or a seasoned hot-pot enthusiast ready to make it at home, the recipes in this book are achievable for all levels of cooks in

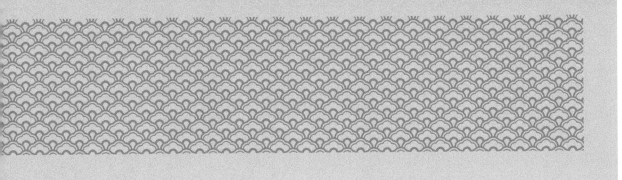

settings that range from weeknight casual to entertaining fun. You will find an introductory chapter with instructions to get started, including a list of ingredients and how long they take to cook, plus recipes with specific combinations from different countries.

The seduction of hot pot boils down to the broth. In this book, I cover popular hot-pot broth flavors from an array of East and Southeast Asian cuisines. I have also included some signature soups that can easily be turned into a hot-pot broth base. With each cultural influence, there are certain ingredients that are commonly enjoyed in those broths, which I've included for best results with each recipe. In cases when ingredients are less familiar or difficult to find, I provide substitutions and resources for where you may buy them. But remember, there is no right or wrong here. Hot pot caters to everyone's tastes. I encourage you to have fun, try new foods, and customize the experience to your preferences. The adventure all lies in the experimenting!

I am excited to share with you the delectable pleasures of hot pot and creating the setting in the comfort of your home. With the growing importance of health, nutrition, and home cooking, there really is no better way to reap these benefits than with hot pot. You get to relish the unique flavors of Asia and a variety of broth profiles that will give you a different experience every time. Let's get started!

CHAPTER ONE

Hot Pot at Home

Hot pot is a well-balanced, one-pot meal that can be adapted to suit any tastes. We'll discuss the components of hot pot step by step here. You'll learn where hot pot originated and where its influence can be found today. You will find recipes from across Asia, including the countries where hot pots are most popular and whose flavors can be replicated simply. Creating the table setting at home is easy and affordable with the right choice of hot pots, essential utensils, and serving dishes. I've also noted regional cooking differences and cooking etiquette to consider for the most authentic hot-pot experience.

WHAT IS HOT POT?

Hot pot is essentially cooking food in intervals by simmering ingredients in a steaming broth. It is best enjoyed with company and is rooted in communal cooking. Prepared plates of thinly sliced raw meats, seafood, vegetables, mushrooms, tofu, and noodles are quickly cooked in a heated hot broth set at the center of the table and ladled into bowls for eating.

Foods can be enjoyed two ways: cooked all together on a stove top or tableside in a hot pot, or in the Chinese-style hot-pot method of cooking for yourself. Here, each guest cooks their choice of foods in the pot or in a ladle, then the items are scooped into their bowl and dipped into a sauce to eat. With that setting, you can imagine the endless combinations, from the flavors in the broth to the ingredients you're cooking and the sauces you dip them in.

Hot pots are referred to by many names, such as Mongolian hot pots, fire pots, steamboats, shabu-shabu (in Japan and Taiwan), *sin-sul-lo* (in Korea), and sukiyaki (in Japan and Laos), to name a few. It is very similar to Western fondue, except the base is a broth and the ingredients used are different. As foods are mostly cooked in their natural state, whether fresh or frozen, it comes down to the flavors and seasonings in the broth. That infusion is what gives the food its delicious taste, which changes up with every different broth. Hot pot is very different from soup, as it's heartier, but still less dense than stew. The best part is how interactive it is—cooking and eating out of a shared vessel with family and friends creates an experience of togetherness.

History and Origins

Steeped in 1,900 years of history, hot pot is profound in Chinese food culture both past and present. The discovery of bronze pots from the Western Han dynasty in ancient China led scholars to believe they were the equivalent of today's hot pot. Scenes of people enjoying hot pot were recorded in stone relief during that period, supporting that hot pot originated at least then. According to archaeological research, wild game such as deer, boar, pheasants, turtles, and even bear and tigers were commonly eaten. The Han people were already cooking with seasonings such as Sichuan pepper, ginger, and scallions. However, it is said that the Mongolians were the ones who popularized this cooking method about 900 years ago.

Legend has it that Genghis Khan's cook had to quickly feed the troops before a battle. Sitting and eating over an open fire, Mongolian warriors and horsemen used their helmets as bowls to simmer the broth with chunks of horse meat and mutton. Subsequently, hot pot spread throughout China where distinct regional variations developed. This practical and effortless cooking style was embraced by both commoners and royals. There was no social prestige involved. The rich might have used higher-quality meat and a greater variety of produce, but the manner of eating from the hot pot was the same. Hot pot's influence made its way into Japan in 1338, known as *nabemono*, and the rest of Asia has since welcomed it in a myriad of forms.

Hot Pot Today

Across Asia, the hot-pot culture is all about community, whether in restaurants or private homes. Most notable is China's Chongqing region in the interior west, known as the hot-pot capital of the world, where it is said one in five restaurants serves hot pot, mainly in their ubiquitous famous style of tongue-numbing spicy *ma la.* Hot pot is not just food or fuel, but a lifestyle for locals. Asian countries beyond China—to the east, Korea and Japan, and to the southeast, Thailand and Cambodia—have adopted this form of cooking, and each has their own unique broths and ingredients. Still the universal setting is the same, bringing family and friends together in a social manner, chatting and bonding while cooking and eating to their hearts' content, often enjoyed with alcohol. That flourishing tradition of community and connection is embodied in the spirit of hot pot.

Regional Differences

A single country can serve varying styles of hot pots depending on what is grown in and available to the different regions. Of the countless types in China, the northern parts (near Beijing) are known for fresh, quality mutton and have less of a broth focus. Toward the south, seafood and vegetables in a lighter broth are characteristic of Cantonese cuisine. In southeastern countries, fragrant lemongrass, lime leaves, and chiles offer tangy, citrusy, and spicy notes that are standard in their broths.

In this book, the diversity of broth and ingredient combinations is well represented in hot-pot styles of China (including Mongolia), Korea, Japan, and Taiwan in the east and Thailand, Laos, Vietnam, Cambodia, the Philippines, and Malaysia in the southeast. I encourage you to kick back and relax with the Chinese hot-pot style of cooking a little food and eating slowly at the table. Take in the setting around you, the sights, aromas, tastes, and conversations that can be had only with a slow and gradual-paced meal.

HOW TO HAVE HOT POT AT HOME

Before you begin cooking, you will need some basic equipment. Many are things you probably already have, such as ladles, eating utensils, bowls, and dishes. The main item to consider is the hot pot out of which you will be cooking. With the many options available, the investment is small, and choosing the right one can give you joyful hot-pot memories for years to come.

Everything you need to know about creating hot pot will be covered in chapter 2. These three key components include the base broth, the ingredients to add and cook in broth and for how long, as well as the sauces used to dip the foods in.

Choosing a Hot Pot

You may already own something that can work, but if not, it's very inexpensive to get started. My go-to is simply a large two-handled 5-quart stainless steel pot with a glass lid over a portable gas burner. At extended family gatherings we usually cook in two electric skillets set at each end of the table, so everyone can have access. For any hot pots or heating equipment with a short plug, you will need an extension cord to keep it out of harm's way. I will outline the most accessible options with tableside dining as the focus and their approximate price range. If you need to buy one, keep in mind the ideal height and diameter of the pot: 3½ to 5 inches deep and at least 12 inches across would feed four to six adults.

Check out your local department stores, kitchenware stores, or Asian houseware stores. Amazon carries an extensive selection, and you can browse models according to customer recommendation reviews. Simply search with "hot pot" as the keyword to see a number of options.

Healthy Hot Pots

Hot pot is the ultimate healthy comfort food. From the vast array of broth bases and wide assortment of ingredients such as lean proteins, vegetables, noodles, and dumplings, there's something for everyone! Poaching delicately in a hot broth preserves the ingredients' natural flavors and imparts flavor into the broth, which gradually becomes more tasty and robust as you cook. Thus, a sip of the delectable brew toward the end is the perfect finish to a satisfying and nourishing meal.

The most basic broth can be made just by cooking chicken bones in water. We all know what wonders homemade chicken soup can do for us. Just a few slices of ginger gives you its benefit as a digestive aid and cold preventer, not to mention flavor. In addition, many hot-pot styles use Chinese medicinal herbs and ingredients to prevent ailments and give you energy, especially during colder months when our immune system needs a boost. For example, dried Chinese red dates (also called jujubes) maintain blood flow and detoxify the liver, goji berries (also called wolf berries) are high in antioxidants and help promote sleep and energy, and the small root of the ginseng is prized for its rejuvenating properties and source of vitality. The bottom line: no matter how you prepare it, hot pot is one of the most natural forms of healthy cooking.

How your hot pot reacts to heat is an important factor in selecting the right one for you. Cooking tableside, you are looking at induction or electric hot plates or a portable gas burner that uses butane cartridges. Induction heat reduces wasted energy, as 90 percent of the energy goes toward the plate's core function and it cooks faster and evenly. The surface does not get hot, so it's not only safer, but spilled food will not get baked onto the cooktop. However, induction heat will only work with cookware made of magnetic steel such as cast iron or stainless steel. Electric hot plates take longer to heat up and the heat distributes unevenly, but they can be used with all cookware and are less expensive. The average price of a single induction plate runs $40 to $50, whereas an electric plate is around $20 to $40.

A **gas-powered hot pot** or portable gas burner is the most practical heating device. Affordable and conveniently cordless, it offers good control of the flame with a temperature dial. Butane cartridges are purchased separately. One will last you two to three hot-pot sessions. A gas burner can be used with all kinds of pots. I picked up the one I have in a Korean store, and it comes with a compact case for easy storage. ($25 to $40)

Clay pots (*donabe*) are a traditional Japanese clay earthenware designed with a rounded bottom and a domed lid with a little hole for steam to escape. The heat is conducted in a gradual, even way, and it works best over an open flame. You can also use other stoneware, ceramic, or Chinese sand pots. To avoid uneven heat distribution, clay pots should not be used on electric hot plates. (Basic 8-inch *donabe*: $45 to $60)

Cast-iron casseroles or Dutch ovens are great alternatives, as they distribute heat efficiently just like *donabe* and are sturdy. Although they get hot quickly, the downside is that they don't retain the heat for long. You can't see how the cooking is going and there's no hole in the lid, but you can let steam escape by inserting a fork between the lid and pot. Stainless steel pots get hot at the point of heat contact but are not nearly as good at circulating the heat. This is what I have been using all along, and it works out fine. (6-quart Dutch oven: $60 to $75)

An **electric hot pot** has a deep dish that fits into a pot, an adjustable temperature control, and a glass lid to see the food cooking. Designed for safe hot potting, some models have a detachable magnetic cord and handles that stay cool when you take the dish out. (12-inch diameter: $60)

An **electric skillet** is a wide shallow vessel that can be round or square. The temperature is controlled by a dial. It's fairly inexpensive, convenient to use, and six to eight people can easily cook around it. (12-inch with glass lid: $35 to $50)

Fondue pots that are more modern can work like a fondue burner with a small butane tank or an alcohol burner that adjusts flame and heat capacity. The most convenient would be an electric fondue pot that comes with a base, bowl, and a temperature knob. If you have one of these already, use it. If not, consider looking at the more suitable options listed here.

I don't recommend cooking with an Instant Pot for hot pot. The tall height of the pot is not convenient to diners, and the heavy lid is cumbersome. Same goes for a slow cooker, as you cannot achieve a boil even when it is set at maximum heat.

Should I Get a Split Pot?

A split pot is a shallow 4-inch-deep hot pot, usually aluminum, with a divider down the middle. These are commonly used for offering two broths simultaneously, a spicy broth in one and non-spicy in the other. They are inexpensive, and recommended if you love changing up the tastes or if family and guests prefer one broth over the other, such as meatless on one side. (12-inch with glass lid: $25 to $40)

Essential Utensils and Dishes

Slotted spoons or spiders: An essential tool to filter out the soup and take out ingredients conveniently, without fishing for them with personal chopsticks. A regular-size slotted spoon or spider would do the common job of scooping out food for everyone.

Other Uses for Your Hot Pot

Cast-iron casseroles, Dutch ovens, stone pots, or *donabe* are great for long slow cooking over the stove such as chilis and stews or braises in the oven. They can also be used for baking bread. Electric hot pots and skillets are versatile for sautéing, stir-frying, and steaming. Some models feature a removable grill or barbecue plate and a steaming rack. Something to think about if you want a multifunctional device that can do more than serve hot-pot meals.

Setting the Table

For tableside cooking, the heated hot pot is placed in the center for all diners to have access. Plates of ingredients with raw meat and vegetables are served separately around the hot pot. Foods can be evenly divided for better reach, especially when entertaining a crowd.

Each table setting should have a shallow bowl for cooked foods and a small serving bowl for sauce. Utensils for each person include a small sieve or scoop ladle and a pair of chopsticks. Shared chopsticks or tongs should be offered alongside the plates for picking up the uncooked foods. Have a soup ladle and soup spoons ready to serve the flavorful broth.

Ladles or hot-pot strainer scoops: Individual metal sieve ladles are convenient to keep food in one place or control cooking times with the diner in charge. They are also convenient for scooping out cooked foods.

Chopsticks: Chopsticks are Asia's cutlery and may take a bit of time to master. Wooden ones are light and easy on the fingers. A regular pair is needed for each diner with separate long chopsticks, if using, to remove cooked foods from the pot.

Bowls: A shallow 5- to 6-inch bowl is perfect for eating meals in rounds and for soup. Enamel is best to retain heat.

Plates or platters: Serve your assorted food selection on several plates or platters. Any shapes work and should be about 10 inches or larger to contain ample food. I like using enamel plates for raw meats and seafood and plastic platters for mounds of leafy vegetables for some presentation contrast. Leave out an empty plate to place cooked foods that have not been claimed by diners.

Tongs: Tongs are useful for lifting larger amounts of food into the broth such as leafy vegetables and noodles.

COOKING AND ETIQUETTE

Sharing a pot with your fellow diners is an intimate experience. Depending how close you are, the approach could be more freestyle, with several ingredients tossed in to cook and everyone taking out what they wish, or diners can cook their own in individual ladles. With my family and friends, I often combine both styles, with diners filling their own separate ladles of foods (often meat that cooks quickly) and larger items like leafy vegetables and longer-cooking items like frozen dumplings or meatballs cooked together in the pot. It is hygienic and respectful to everyone at the table not to use the eating chopsticks to pick out food. Use your ladle or designated serving chopsticks for this. It is customary to place your eating chopsticks across your bowl when you are finished.

Cooking While Eating or Before Serving

In parts of Asia, such as Korea and Japan, the customary way to eat hot pot is to put a bunch of ingredients in broth, let them come to a boil, and leave simmering while food is ladled out to eat. It is mainly in China and Taiwan where ladles are regularly used for diners to cook themselves. This style is also enjoyed in many Southeast Asian countries. Congregating, leisurely grazing, and socializing over hot pot is what it's about. These methods favor a slow-paced enjoyment of cooking gradually and eating together.

A common etiquette across Asian cultures is that we wait for the elder at the table to begin eating to commence the meal. Cultural etiquette nuances are interesting to note. In Japan, the person who sits nearest to the hot pot should put in the ingredients and observe cooking times. To show appreciation for the meal, it is customary to noisily slurp your noodles and soup. In Korea, however, it is the opposite. Lifting your bowl to eat or drink soup is considered impolite. Both chopsticks and a spoon are necessary utensils for each diner. While noodles are served with most Asian hot-pot meals, an accompanying bowl of steamed rice is a must in Japan and Vietnam.

The important communal aspect draws on the simple symbolism of "roundness." In Chinese and Taiwanese culture, the "yuan" circle means reunion and unity and is greatly presented in the hot-pot setting. When eating hot pot, a round pot is centered at the table with lots of food and everyone around it, and often that table is round as well. In addition, the burning fire and upward steam symbolizes flourishing life. Therefore, hot pot is a common tradition at Chinese New Year's Eve family reunion dinners with plentiful dishes and a crowded table to celebrate abundance and prosperity.

Keep the Meat and Veggies Separate

Meats and vegetables should always be kept separate to avoid salmonella and cross contamination. It is a good idea to serve raw meat and seafood on small plates and refill as you run out, with extras already prepared in the refrigerator, as it is important to keep raw foods safe throughout the meal.

Everything Has a Cook Time

Whether you are cooking foods all together before serving or cooking as you eat, always prepare it with the ingredients' cook time in mind. Cooking at once involves layering the foods in the broth according to what takes longer to cook first. For example, with frozen dumplings or fish balls, put these in with a cook time of five minutes in the simmering broth. Three minutes in, you may want to add kabocha squash and carrots that take two minutes to cook; then shrimp, tofu, and watercress bunches at one to two minutes, and leafy vegetables and thinly sliced meat around the 1-minute to 30-second mark. Then all your ingredients are cooked together and taken out in one shot. Just don't overcrowd your pot and be sure to keep the broth at a simmer. At some points, you may want to cover the pot to return the broth to a boil. This is where a see-through lid comes in handy. A good rule of thumb is when in doubt, whether it's cooked or not, you can let it simmer a little longer.

For cooking, after the initial boil, you'll want the heat turned down to medium so that your hot pot simmers. It is necessary to have extra broth on hand or a kettle of hot water to replenish the broth. Since the broth is getting more concentrated as you're cooking, plain water is usually fine without diluting flavors too much. You will read about the categories of ingredients and their specific cook times in chapter 2.

What to Do with Leftovers

One of the great joys of hot pot is the sight of heaping platters of foods. The plentiful presentation catches our attention as plates are brought out to the table one after another, opening up our appetite. In the likelihood that leftovers remain, the broth and both cooked and uncooked ingredients can be eaten the next day.

My favorite way to serve leftovers is to turn them into a pot of noodle soup. I add water to top up the broth, bring it to a boil, adjust the seasonings, add raw ingredients according to their cook times, and during the last minute or so add any leftover cooked foods to heat through along with prepared noodles. Alternatively, you can cook the ingredients in the broth and serve them with a side bowl of steamed rice. The meat and vegetables are great in a stir-fry with a bit of chopped garlic and soy sauce to season.

Keep It Fun!

Encourage your diners to try a little of everything and to sip the delicious broth at the end of the meal! Raise your glass for a quick toast, and cook, dip, and eat to your hearts' content. Hot pot doesn't have to be a serious affair. Enjoy the fun!

CHAPTER TWO

Everything You Need to Enjoy Hot Pot

Hot-pot assembly is about balancing flavors and textures with ingredients that bestow nutrition, contrast, and harmony. Learn about the wide array of hot-pot staples and ingredient favorites, including where to buy and alternatives if you can't find them or get to an Asian grocery store. Explore what is involved in making your own broth, popular condiments to create your own dipping sauces, and of course the multitude of common and interesting ingredients to enjoy hot pot.

WHERE AND HOW TO SHOP

When shopping for the right tools and ingredients for hot pot, your first bet is to visit an Asian food market. There are import and specialty food shops that might be helpful as well for those harder-to-find condiments and dried goods. This may be an Asian gourmet store or a trading food company that is opened to the public. Otherwise, larger supermarkets that carry Asian produce and a decent condiment section will cover what you need. The great thing about hot pot is that the ingredients can be flexible; if you can't find something you're looking for, like a Japanese kabocha squash, another ingredient with a similar flavor or texture, like a sweet potato, will work.

Use fresh produce that is in season and at its best. If you are looking to cook a specific hot-pot style, such as Korean, check out a Korean grocer if there's one around you. You will find a core selection of meat, vegetables, and seasonings that are foundational to that country's cuisine. Check out and support the small stores in your area that carry and deliver Asian products, even for things like frozen dumplings and fish balls, which are classic hot-pot favorites. Alternatively, many stores nowadays offer online shopping, so you can have harder-to-find ingredients shipped to your home.

What If I Can't Get to an Asian Grocery Store?

You can make an excellent hot pot with ingredients that are available in supermarkets and online. Making a tasty homemade broth can be as simple as cooking with a whole small chicken or chicken bones, or a handful of mushrooms and diced tomatoes. Many vegetables (both leafy and root), mushrooms, meat, noodles, and dried goods are widely available. Frozen seafood, such as shrimp and calamari, can be found in any supermarket. And you can slice up your own meat for quick cooking by par-freezing your meat before cutting.

You can also substitute easy-to-find ingredients for many specialty items, and I've suggested substitutions throughout the book. A vegetable as simple as iceberg or green leaf lettuce adds good texture to hot pot if you can't find a particular Asian green. In the end, hot pot can be achievable and easy and can make use of whatever ingredients are available to you.

MAKING BROTH

Creating your own broth is fairly simple to do, whether you buy a packaged seasoning packet or make your own from scratch. Here are some of my favorite approaches that will each serve you well in a variety of recipes in this book.

Powdered Broths and Seasoning Packets

These handy flavor bases are widely available in Asian supermarkets and online and help you create your hot-pot broth instantly. Powdered broths range from mushroom or vegetable to chicken and fish. For true convenience, buy hot-pot soup-base products. They come in a packet, pouch, or pod container and can be powdered, concentrated liquid, or paste. These complex soup bases contain harder-to-find seasonings and ingredients and many even make a restaurant's secret blend conveniently available to home cooks. With instructions on the package, they offer foolproof convenience: just dissolve the ingredients and simmer in water. (Some also ask you to add a few common ingredients to accentuate flavors, such as garlic and scallions.)

I recommend Lee Kum Kee, a reputable Chinese condiment company that offers a good selection of hot-pot broths in satay, seafood, and spicy Sichuan flavors conveniently concentrated in a liquid pouch. Another great brand comes from the world-famous, 300-restaurant chain Little Sheep Hot Pot, which offers spicy and non-spicy broth flavors. Dozens of herbs go into the soup base alone, and the company says it is so unique and flavorful that dipping sauce is not required.

Making Stock

Rich meat stocks are generally made inexpensively with bones. Check out your local butchers and Asian meat counters, and if you don't see them displayed, ask the staff if they have any set aside. I have also found them packaged fresh and frozen in Asian supermarkets. Pork neck and back bones are good choices to make pork broth, as they are meatier than other bones, which adds to the broth's depth of flavor. Use chicken carcasses or a small whole chicken (after cooking, you can shred the meat to eat with the soup), beef bones such as legs, shins, and knuckles with a little marrow for richer flavor, and lamb bones.

Always blanch bones for about 5 minutes first, to rid them of impurities. I do this with a few slices of ginger to also get rid of any meat smells. Discard the water, rinse the bones thoroughly in cold water, and then hard simmer them in water for an average of 1½ hours. Fish stock is usually made by stir-frying, then simmering, fish heads, bones, or skin-on pieces of fish with ginger slices until the broth is milky white (whole smelts are great for this), but you can also simply simmer a handful of dried anchovies or pick up prepared stock at your supermarket. Premade broths in cans or cartons (which are often prepared with Western ingredients such as onions, celery, and carrots) can work, but the brands Knorr and Swanson also offer chicken broth in cans (identified with Chinese writing on the label) that have savory seasonings that work better in Asian hot pots.

Vegetarian and Vegan Broths

The usual base ingredients for vegetarian broth include dried shiitake mushrooms, kombu, miso or *doenjang* soybean paste, kimchi, tomatoes, or coconut milk (which adds a creamy heartiness for Southeast Asian hot pots). This involves simmering the ingredients until flavor is rendered, dissolving the paste, or adding aromatics and seasonings to coconut milk. You can use a mushroom- or vegetable-based broth powder for a simple broth base. Canned vegetarian broths made with a medley of veggies are widely available at the stores. Choosing a version with Asian flavorings is ideal but not necessary.

Getting the Seasonings and Flavor Right

Spices offer aromatic layers of flavor, color, and texture that work in tandem to balance and play off each other's distinct characteristics. Oils add body and textured mouthfeel, such as silkiness to tofu and velvety richness to meats. Bolder broth compositions with spices and oil develop more depth of flavor as you're cooking and can be heartier and more satisfying.

My suggestion for preparing the broth recipes in this book for the first time is to follow the lower range of seasonings and spices in the ingredient list, then taste and adjust accordingly. It is always easier to add seasoning than to dilute with water or broth and have to rebuild the intended flavors up again! Especially with spicy broths, start low, then make note of how much you ended up using for next time.

Some common ingredients you may have or might want to try: Bay leaves impart a woodsy flavor, as do cinnamon sticks with a sweet and slightly warm citrusy note. Both should be removed from the broth before serving. Sichuan peppercorn (a.k.a. prickly ash) with its lemony overtone and numbing tongue-tingling quality works in tandem with spicy Sichuan facing heaven chiles to create the renowned spicy-tingly *ma la tang* (soup) profile; miso paste made from fermented soybeans creates a quick healthy broth base, and fish sauce (fermented anchovies or sardines) imparts a unique savory tang and saltiness. Cooking wine is usually salted and made from fermented rice used in everyday cooking. A popular variety is Shaoxing, which is amber in color, slightly vinegary, and rich in taste. If you can't find Shaoxing, dry sherry is a good substitute.

DIPPING SAUCES AND VINEGARS

Sauces impart a finesse to your meal just before you eat it. If you are cooking with a simple or mild broth, sauces also offer a flavor boost. The most commonly used ingredients, which you can enjoy with a wide variety of Asian hot pots, are a good all-purpose naturally brewed soy sauce as the main base (I like Pearl River Bridge brand); rice vinegar for tang and lift to counter the heaviness of meat; *shacha* (*sa cha*) sauce made from oil, garlic, shallots, chiles, and seafood, which is intensely savory with a grilled taste; sesame oil as a finishing aromatic nutty oil to add body; tahini sesame paste or peanut butter adds creamy nuttiness; sambal oelek made with red chiles, vinegar, and oil as a fiery addition to dips; and wasabi/hot mustard sold in tubes or alternatively Dijon mustard for pungent heat. Combine your favorite flavors—a little bit of this and that—in your dipping sauce to elevate the tastes of your cooked foods.

GARNISHES

Garnishes are the final touch and flavor accent to the ingredients simmering in the hot pot. Most commonly served with Japanese hot pots, they are often an addition to dipping sauces and meant to be sprinkled on just before eating. You can also add these directly to your dipping sauce for textural vibrancy. I like to set out garnishes such as sliced scallions, chopped cilantro, garlic, and chiles with any sauce or condiments, so diners can mix and match to create their own blend.

Which garnishes should you use? Scallions refresh the palate with a touch of sharpness to balance bold-flavored foods. Cilantro gives food an herbaceous zing. Aromatic garlic is super delicious and complementary for all foods, and chiles brighten with heat punch. Anise-flavored Thai basil leaves accent Southeast Asian hot pots. White or black sesame seeds add visual texture. Red pepper flakes or ground cayenne pepper give food a spicy pop. A sprinkle of ground black or white pepper goes well with meats. Thinly shredded nori seaweed pairs nicely with seafood or tofu in a Japanese hot pot.

MAIN INGREDIENTS

Now, for the stars of the show. You can cook a wide variety of foods in your hot-pot broth, including vegetables, mushrooms, meat, dumplings, and noodles, and they can range from the most common, such as spinach and beef, to the gourmet and exotic, like oysters and offal. In my recipes, I focus on the more familiar items to make the hot-pot combinations approachable, but feel free to add any unique or special items you like. Fresh or frozen ingredients are always best, but in a pinch canned ingredients can work nicely. Here are some of the most common types of ingredients I use in my hot pots:

Tofu and Soy Products

Tofu: Also known as bean curd, tofu is produced from the milky liquid from crushed soy beans that is coagulated and pressed in a process similar to making cheese. Tofu makes a great meat substitute in vegetarian hot pots but is also great alongside other proteins.

Blocks of tofu are available in water-filled packages labeled silken, soft, medium, and firm in the refrigerated section of the grocery store. Soft is the most popular texture because it is smooth and soaks up flavor well. Medium and firm hold up better when handling with the rest of the hot-pot ingredients. For soft tofu, cut the block into 1-inch cubes, and let them drain in a colander for 15 minutes to release excess moisture. Cooking tofu takes 1 minute.

Tofu Skin: This is the thin, rich layer of soy protein that forms on the surface of boiling soy milk. The skin is dried and sold in long, thin strips that have a slightly chewy texture and soak up the broth flavors when cooked. Break into 3-inch pieces, hydrate in water for 3 hours, and cook for 2 minutes to soften.

Fried Tofu: There are two common kinds: dense and airy textures. Dense tofu is packaged in bite-size triangles or squares and a block form (to be cut into bite-size pieces). The other kind, square, golden puffs of fried tofu, are light and airy inside. Both are precooked and need only 1 minute in the hot pot. Like tofu skin, puffs absorb the broth flavors well. Just be careful when you bite into them—they can be hot soup bombs!

Tofu Fish Cakes: These are sold in packages alongside fish and meatballs in the freezer section, and are often a blend of tofu and fish shaped into squares or fish. No need to thaw first, but cook these a little longer, 2 to 3 minutes.

Noodles

Noodles are available in many forms, but the most popular for hot pots are made from wheat, rice, mung beans, or *konnyaku* (a plant similar to taro). These noodles can be found fresh, frozen, or dried. If you're in a pinch, pasta noodles such as fettuccine or vermicelli will work fine. Noodles are customarily served at the end with the broth, which has become a rich, flavorful soup, as a way of completing the meal.

Udon: These are thick wheat noodles sold both frozen and on the shelf in the dried-noodle aisle. Hearty and filling, they get well coated with the broth. Cook separately ahead of time, until al dente, so that they just need to be heated through.

Ramen: Made out of egg and wheat, these noodles are sold in fresh, frozen, and instant formats. They cook quickly in steaming broth—about 2 minutes. You can cook frozen ramen directly in the pot. If you are using instant noodle packages, just use the noodles and discard the seasoning packets unless specified.

Soba: Also known as buckwheat, these noodles are usually packaged in portioned serving bundles, are bespeckled, and can range in color from light to dark brown. They have a distinct nutty flavor and 1 cup contains a high 6 percent vegetable protein and vitamins B_1 and B_2. To maximize its nutrition, look for brands made with 100 percent buckwheat. Popular in Japanese cuisine, they need to cook first, until al dente, and should be rinsed several times in water to remove excess starch. In the hot pot, they only need to be warmed through.

Rice Noodles: When dried, these come in different thicknesses, from thin vermicelli to medium. Fresh rice noodles, also known as *ho fun* (medium-wide) can be found in the refrigerated section of most large Asian markets. Cook dried noodles according to the directions on the package, and blanch fresh noodles in hot water ahead of time to separate them. Drain well.

Mung Bean Noodles: Also called cellophane noodles, these are made from green mung beans, are sold dried, and often come in single-portion bundles in a package. These cook directly in the hot pot for a mere minute, loosened in the broth with chopsticks.

***Konnyaku*:** This is sold in different formats and can be translucent to bespeckled grey, gelatinous, and sold in packages filled with salted water. The ones I prefer are white thin strands (called *shirataki*) or small knotted *konnyaku* bundles. Calorie-free, very low-carb, high in dietary fiber, and containing 97 percent water, *konnyaku* is considered a great diet food in Japan and China. It cooks in 1 minute.

Common Ingredients

Button Mushrooms: Halve and cook for 1 minute.

Carrots: Peel and slice on an angle into ½-inch pieces and cook for 2 minutes.

Celery: Peel and slice on an angle into ½-inch pieces and cook for 1 minute.

Cruciferous Vegetables (Broccoli, Cauliflower): Cut into 2-inch florets and cook for 1 minute.

Green Leafy Lettuce or Iceberg Lettuce: Cut into 3-inch pieces and cook for 30 seconds.

Hot Dogs: Cut into bite-size pieces and cook for 1 to 2 minutes.

Leeks: Remove green parts, slice on an angle into ½-inch pieces and rinse well to remove sand; cook for 1 to 2 minutes.

Pineapple Chunks: Use fresh or canned pineapple chunks and cook for 30 seconds.

Spam: Slice into bite-size pieces and cook for 1 to 2 minutes.

Tomatoes: Cut into wedges and cook for 2 minutes.

Leaves and Stems

Green vegetables are easy to add to the hot-pot table and impart great flavor to broths. They balance out a meal's textures and colors and bring in the freshness of what's in season—and they add lots of nutrition.

Asian Chives: Popular in Chinese and Korean cuisines, this long, green-stem vegetable is sold in bundles. The taste is a cross between scallions and garlic. Used chopped in the dumpling recipes; you can also add 3-inch pieces to broths for extra flavor.

Bamboo Shoots: Buy packaged whole poached shoots sold in the refrigerated section. These taste better than canned, but ready-to-use canned versions are more readily available and can be found as whole, sliced, or slivered shoots. Whole shoots are ideal; you can thinly slice them yourself after rinsing in cold water and draining. Bamboo shoots cook in 1 to 2 minutes.

Bean Sprouts: These grow from sprouted mung beans and are used extensively across Asian cuisines. In hot pots, they cook in a mere 30 seconds.

Bok Choy: This classic Chinese vegetable with long crisp stalks and green spinach-like leaves is a hot-pot favorite. There is another type, Shanghai bok choy, which is green throughout. Both are also sold in a more tender baby variety. Heads of bok choy can be prepped with the outer large leaves sliced in half and the tender middle sliced lengthwise to keep it intact, and it cooks in 1 minute.

Mat Kimchi: Kimchi is a Korean fermented vegetable side dish made from a variety of vegetables such as napa cabbage and daikon radishes. *"Mat"* kimchi simply means cut kimchi. Once opened, kimchi should be refrigerated so that it lasts longer.

Napa Cabbage: One of the most popular vegetables for hot pot, napa cabbage (also known as Chinese cabbage) has white stems, tightly packed pale green leaves, and a mild taste. Its porous leaves work like a sponge to soak up flavors. To prepare them, separate the leaves and cut into 2-inch pieces. These cook quickly, in 1 minute.

Spinach: You can use convenient, prewashed baby spinach or regular spinach sold in bunches for hot pot. Ensure the roots are trimmed off but keep the stems intact. Spinach cooks in less than 30 seconds.

Watercress: One of my favorite greens, watercress has small, rounded green leaves on thin stems, is sold in bunches, and tastes slightly peppery. Loosen the bunches and cook small handfuls for about 2 minutes. They impart a wonderful, sweet flavor to broths.

Mushrooms

Mushrooms contribute a hearty, meaty texture to the hot pot, and many hot-pot meals will have a variety of different types. Low in calories and rich in protein, mushrooms add an earthy flavor to the broth and impart lots of umami richness. You can use any type of fresh mushrooms you like, but following are some of the most popular options for hot pot. Most mushrooms cook in 1 minute.

Enoki: White, delicate, and light, enokis come in bunches and should be separated. These are popular in Japanese and Korean hot pots and cook quickly, in 30 seconds.

King Oyster: With tan caps and thick stems, king oyster mushrooms have a rich umami flavor and meaty texture. Cut lengthwise into ½-inch pieces.

Oyster Mushrooms: These are delicate mushrooms with irregularly shaped caps that add earthy flavor and fragrance. Cut them into pieces if they are too large.

Shiitake: Use fresh shiitake mushrooms whole or, if large, cut in half; they cook in about 2 minutes. Dried shiitakes, which can be purchased in Asian markets, are more concentrated than fresh and add distinct richness to the broth. Dried mushrooms should be rehydrated: soak them in warm water for 4 hours, and discard the woody stem. Cook for 5 minutes in the hot pot to also allow flavors to seep into the broth.

Shimeji: This Japanese mushroom is also known as a beech mushroom and grows in tight clusters of white stems with brown or white caps. Separate them into smaller bunches, which will offer a robust texture to the hot pot.

Straw Mushrooms: Straw mushrooms have small tan compact caps and thin stems and are a good option for canned mushrooms. Drain and rinse to use.

Root Vegetables

Roots and tubers add heft and al dente texture to hot pot. They also pair well with meat and tofu for heartiness. Cook these for just a short time to avoid a mushy texture.

Daikon: These large radishes are white with a green tinge and resemble a giant carrot. They are popular in Chinese, Japanese, and Korean hot-pot dishes. When poached, they develop a delicate sweetness, and they readily absorb hot-pot flavors. Peeled and sliced into ½-inch rounds or moons, these cook for 2 minutes.

Kabocha Squash: This is a popular Japanese pumpkin with a tough, dark green skin with defined ridges. The flesh has a dense texture and is buttery yellow to bright orange. To prepare, cut the kabocha in half, peel, and seed it, then cut into ¾-inch segments. You can use sweet potato or pumpkin as a substitute. Cook for 2 minutes.

Lotus Root: Crunchy lotus root is a tuber with large holes running through its center. Peel and slice crosswise into ½-inch rounds. Some stores offer frozen lotus root already sliced. Cook for 2 minutes.

Fish Balls and Meat Balls

Fish balls are like meatballs but are less dense. They have a smooth texture and are always a popular hot-pot ingredient. They are made with a variety of seafood such as fish, cuttlefish, shrimp, octopus, imitation crab, and lobster and can be shaped into balls and fried, or formed into cylinders or flat rectangles called fish cakes (popular in Japanese and Korean stores). You can also find packages of assorted fish balls specially designed for Japanese *oden* (stew).

Any Asian supermarket will have a frozen assortment, with some places offering fresh. Fish or seafood balls tend to be smooth and springy, whereas meatballs are denser and more toothsome. If you find fresh seasoned fish paste sold in a tub (which is often made of dace fish), an easy way to form a fish dumpling is to scoop some paste with a teaspoon and slide it out with another spoon to create an oval shape. Frozen fish balls do not need to be defrosted before use. Cook fresh for 3 minutes and frozen for 5 minutes before eating.

Meatballs are also popular. They are made with chicken, pork, or beef and can be found frozen or in the refrigerated section. Beef balls are often served with Vietnamese beef noodle pho soup; if you can find ones with tendon, these are the most bouncy and flavorful. Cook frozen meatballs for 5 minutes and fresh meatballs for 3 minutes.

Dumplings

Asian dumplings of all kinds are becoming more widely available in all kinds of stores, usually in the freezer section. A well-stocked Asian supermarket will have a broader selection, including popular versions filled with pork, pork and vegetables (such as leeks, napa cabbage, or chives), and beef. Look for dumplings that are meant to be boiled in water, as there are also versions made for panfrying, such as Japanese gyoza. You can often find vegetable- and kimchi-filled dumplings in Korean supermarkets. Wontons are soup dumplings that have a thinner, more translucent skin and are commonly filled with pork or pork and shrimp. You can cook frozen wontons directly in the hot pot for 3 minutes, and dumplings for about 5 minutes. They are ready when they float to the surface.

Eggs

Chicken eggs can be boiled ahead and peeled. You can also do that for cute, tiny quail eggs, which are popular in hot pots. Alternatively, look for cooked quail eggs in cans; drain and rinse before use. A beaten egg is commonly added to dipping sauces for Chinese and Japanese hot pot as an accompaniment to temper the heat and impart silkiness to foods. For raw use, the U.S. Food and Drug Administration recommends using pasteurized eggs since they are less at risk of containing salmonella.

Other Dry Goods

These specialty ingredients are found in Asian supermarkets and specialty food shops.

Seaweed: For hot-pot broths, look for dried kelp (kombu), an edible umami-rich deep ocean seaweed used to create Japanese dashi—the base of Japanese stock and Korean broths. Kombu is best soaked in room-temperature water, then simmered briefly. (If you cook it too long, the broth will turn slimy; discard the kombu after cooking.) Another type of seaweed is wakame. Buy these dried and precut to add texture. Hydrate in the broth to enjoy in 1 minute.

Seitan: Also known as wheat gluten, this ingredient is a cooked, ready-to-eat, plant-based food made from vital wheat gluten. It is an alternative to soybean-based foods and sometimes used as a meat analogue. Some types of seitan have a chewy or stringy texture that resembles meat more than other substitutes. Great for a vegetarian diet, it is high in protein and versatile in a wide range of meatless recipes. It can be refrigerated in packages, canned, or jarred (the latter two should be drained first). I prefer the fresh kind. These will cook in just 1 to 2 minutes.

Rice Cakes: This ingredient, made from glutinous and non-glutinous rice flours, is shaped into firm cylinders or thin ovals, and can be found both frozen and fresh. These are popular in Korean and Chinese cuisines and add a chewy deliciousness to hot pot. Separate the pieces, and cook them for 5 to 7 minutes, until they plump up. (Seitan is a good substitution for texture.)

SEAFOOD, MEAT, AND POULTRY

Popular hot-pot proteins include a wide variety of seafood and meats. Fish and shellfish impart briny sweetness; chicken gives a light savory taste; while beef, pork, and lamb bestow richer flavors. Cut into bite-size pieces or thinly sliced, these ingredients cook quickly, about 30 seconds for meat and 2 minutes for seafood.

Meats are certainly interchangeable in these recipes; for instance, beef can replace lamb, and you shouldn't worry about getting exactly the right cut. As long as meats are thinly sliced, most cuts will work in hot pot.

The Importance of Thinly Sliced Meat

In Asian supermarkets, you'll find frozen presliced packages of meat that are conveniently designed for hot pots. Thinly sliced meats can be found rolled into frozen cylinders, which makes it easy to remove them for use. You may also be able to buy raw meat that is already shaved thin or ask your butcher to cut it for you.

While these options are convenient, you can easily slice the meat yourself: Freeze for 2 to 3 hours or until the meat is firm enough. To get a slice as thin as possible, make sure your knife is very sharp. It is much easier to slice thinly when the meat is semi-frozen. If it is large, section it into manageable pieces, and always slice against the grain. Or use a mandolin with pieces that fit inside the hand guard. Lay the slices slightly overlapping each other on a plate, cover, and refrigerate until serving.

Fish

When choosing fish for hot pot, boneless fillets are best. Fresh skinless salmon is popular. Frozen white fish fillets are also convenient, and flaky basa, cod, and snapper are often sold boneless, making them very practical to use. Avoid oily fish, such as mackerel, sardines, or anchovies (though dried specimens are sometimes used for making broth). If you buy frozen fish fillets, thaw and drain well before use. Cut all pieces of fish into two-bite pieces; these take less than a minute to cook.

I've had a whole fresh-caught fish cooked in hot pot (*lẩu*) in Vietnam, but this is less typical. If you want to try it, scale the fish, rinse well, remove the fins, and simmer it in your hot pot until fully cooked. Carefully remove it, whole, onto a plate before adding other ingredients to your hot pot. This method creates an instant, delicious fish broth—and, of course, you get to eat the fish, too!

Shellfish

Many kinds of shellfish are popular in hot pots. Shrimp offer a sweet flavor and slightly chewy texture (I like using black tiger shrimp, which are firm). These cook for about 2 minutes or until they are opaque and firm. Squid, with the tentacles separated and the body cut into ½-inch rings, and calamari rings both offer interesting texture and cook for about 1 minute, until opaque. Medium-size scallops, which are nicely sweet, and imitation crab meat (surimi) cut into bite-size pieces, both cook for 30 seconds. Mussels and clams, which are rich and briny, can be used whole or on the half shell for mussels. If whole, look for ones that close after you tap on their shells; they should also feel heavy for their size. Cook for less than 2 minutes and discard the ones that don't open.

Wash and rinse all of your thawed seafood with cold water and salt to clean thoroughly, then drain before use. Be careful not to overcook seafood, or the texture will be rubbery.

Poultry

Chicken wings, sliced chicken breast, and thigh meat are popular poultry cuts to use in hot pot. These do not have to be thinly sliced; bite-size slices are typical and cook in 2 minutes. Whole wings should be cut at the joints for ease of eating. Wing tips can be removed and frozen to make chicken stock.

Beef

The best beef cuts for hot pot are brisket, sirloin, top blade, and chuck. The meat should be firm, finely textured and red. If these are not available, look for anything with a good marbling for tenderness. Thinly sliced, all these cuts should cook in 30 seconds.

Pork

Thinly sliced pork shoulder, butt, and jowl are popular for their tenderness. Koreans love to use pork belly in hot pots; it's sold pre-cut in Korean markets. Cook all of your pork pieces until they have no trace of pink; this should take less than 1 minute.

Lamb

Thinly sliced shoulder or leg is the more tender ideal part of lamb to use. You may need to look for this at a specialty meat counter; however, in Asian supermarkets they are readily available frozen, thinly sliced for this purpose. These cook in 30 seconds. Mutton is a beloved hot-pot meat for its strong gamey taste that complements spicier broths.

ABOUT THE RECIPES

You will find 13 broth recipes in chapter 3 that cover a range of popular Asian broths commonly used in hot pots or that have been adapted from soups. Broth recipes serve up to 8 people. Note that the hot pot recipes serve 4, and you can double the ingredients to serve 8. I recommend cooking 12 to 14 cups of broth to start, with the remaining broth used to replenish the pot as needed.

Everything has a cook time, and whether you are cooking foods all together before serving or cooking as you eat, always prepare hot pot with the ingredients' cook time in mind. The recipes are focused on tableside cooking, with my favorite combinations in each themed hot pot. Try serving with my suggested dipping sauces or create your own.

Chapter 4 will have recipes for some delicious dipping sauces and ingredients, such as dumplings, meatballs, and marinated fish. In chapters 5 and 6, complete recipes with broth and ingredient combinations are provided. These recipes are labeled with their country of origin and with labels that place them in an identifiable category of use. Feel free to adjust recipes as needed. These are only guidelines that show the best-suited ingredients for that broth. Get creative, mix and match, and experiment!

DASHI BROTH, PAGE 40

Broths

ALL-PURPOSE SIMPLE CHICKEN BROTH

GLUTEN-FREE, MEAT

MAKES 20 CUPS | PREP TIME: 15 minutes | COOK TIME: 1½ to 2 hours

Chicken is the most versatile meat broth base suitable for any style of hot pot. This golden broth is multipurpose and is called for as a base broth starter in the subsequent recipes. Dried goji berries (high in antioxidants) and red dates (maintain blood circulation) are invaluable ingredients in traditional Chinese medicine for health benefits and to impart sweetness. If you are using this chicken broth recipe as a base, omit them.

33 cups cold water, divided

4 pounds chicken bones, or 2 chicken carcasses (skin and excess fat removed)

5 peeled (1½-inch-wide and ¼-inch-thick) ginger slices, divided

3 scallions, both white and green parts, cut into 3-inch pieces

2 tablespoons dried goji berries (optional)

8 dried Chinese red dates (optional)

1. Fill a large stockpot with 12 cups of water and bring to a boil. Place the chicken bones into the water.

2. Add 2 slices of ginger and cook for 5 minutes to blanch the bones to remove impurities.

3. Drain and rinse bones thoroughly with cold water.

4. Rinse and wipe the stockpot, then fill it with the remaining 21 cups of water. Add the chicken bones, remaining 3 slices of ginger, the scallions, goji berries (if using), and dates (if using).

5. Bring to a boil, partially covered, then simmer over low heat for 1½ to 2 hours. Skim off any scum and excess oil that floats to the surface.

6. Strain through a sieve into another large pot.

7. Refrigerate the broth in an airtight container for up to 5 days or freeze for up to 3 months.

SUBSTITUTION: Use 4 pounds chicken wings, chicken legs, or a small whole chicken. Cook for 1 hour. Shred the chicken to serve the meat alongside the hot pot.

FRAGRANT MIXED MUSHROOM BROTH

CHINESE, GLUTEN-FREE, MEATLESS, SPICY

MAKES 20 CUPS | PREP TIME: 4 hours (for soaking) | COOK TIME: 35 minutes

This fresh and fragrant Chinese hot-pot style from Yunnan uses foraged mushrooms. We're using dried mushrooms with more earthiness and umami than fresh ones. In Yunnan, flowers and/or mint are typically included. We won't add flowers here, but do try adding fresh mint for a layer of cool sweetness.

12 dried whole shiitake mushrooms

3 cups warm water, divided

30 grams dried porcini mushrooms

17 cups cold water

2 peeled (1½-inch-wide and ¼-inch-thick) ginger slices

3 scallions, both white and green parts, cut into 3-inch pieces

12 dried Chinese red dates

1 to 3 teaspoons Sichuan peppercorns (optional)

3 to 6 Sichuan facing heaven chiles (optional)

2 to 3 tablespoons mushroom or vegetable broth mix powder

Handful fresh mint leaves (optional)

3 large tomatoes, each cut into 8 wedges

Salt

1. In a medium bowl, soak the shiitake mushrooms in 2 cups of warm water for 4 hours. In another bowl, soak the porcini mushrooms in the remaining 1 cup of warm water for 1 hour. Reserve the soaking liquids.

2. In a stockpot, combine the cold water, ginger, scallions, dates, Sichuan peppercorns (if using), and chiles (if using). Add the reserved mushroom liquids, straining any debris, and broth mix powder. Stir and bring to a boil. Turn the heat down to medium and simmer for 30 minutes.

3. Add the mint leaves (if using) during the last 5 minutes of cooking.

4. Remove the whole mushrooms and cut off the stems. Strain and discard the aromatics from the broth. Transfer the broth base into the hot pot.

5. Add the mushroom caps and the tomato and simmer for 5 minutes more. Season with salt to taste.

6. Refrigerate the broth in an airtight container for up to 5 days or freeze for up to 3 months.

PORK BONE BROTH

GLUTEN-FREE, MEAT

MAKES 20 CUPS | PREP TIME: 15 minutes | COOK TIME: 2 hours

This is my very favorite broth for hot pot. It's primarily made with pork bones, but I also add chicken bones in a 2:1 ratio. Growing up, my mother always combined these in her soups so that the flavors played off each other. Chicken imparts sweetness that complements pork's meaty flavor, and the resulting broth tastes sweet and hearty. Always blanch and rinse the pork bones thoroughly of coagulated blood and impurities. This will create a clear, pale, rather than a dark, broth.

33 cups cold water, divided

3 pounds pork back or neck bones (I look for meaty pieces)

4 peeled (1½-inch-wide and ¼-inch-thick) ginger slices, divided

1½ pounds chicken bones, or 1 chicken carcass (skin and excess fat removed)

1 large onion, chopped

1. Fill a large stockpot with 12 cups of water and bring to a boil. Place the pork bones in the water.

2. Add 2 slices of ginger and cook for 5 minutes to blanch the bones to remove impurities.

3. Drain and rinse the bones thoroughly with cold water.

4. Rinse and wipe the stockpot then fill it with the remaining 21 cups of water. Add the pork and chicken bones, the remaining 2 slices of ginger, and the onion. Bring to a boil, partially covered, then simmer over low heat for 2 hours. Skim off any scum that floats to the surface.

5. Remove the pork bones then strain through a sieve into another large pot.

6. Refrigerate the broth in an airtight container for up to 5 days or freeze for up to 3 months.

VARIATION: Remove cooked pork from the bones and serve with soy sauce mixed with a little sesame oil.

SPICY AND TINGLY *MA LA* BROTH

45 MINUTES OR LESS, CHINESE, MEATLESS, SPICY
MAKES 20 CUPS | PREP TIME: 10 minutes | COOK TIME: 30 minutes

Ma la or *ma lat* in Chinese translates to "numbing spicy," which is exactly what Sichuan chiles and peppercorns evoke on your taste buds. Revered in Chongqing, China, this beloved spicy broth is served at hot-pot restaurants filled to the brim with red chiles. Coupled with the numb-tingling sensation left on your tongue from the Sichuan peppercorns, it makes for a rich, bold, and fiery eating experience.

¼ to ½ cup neutral cooking oil

¼ to ½ cup Sichuan hot bean sauce (*doubanjiang* or Chinese chile bean paste)

12 to 15 garlic cloves, coarsely chopped

6 scallions, both green and white parts, cut into 3-inch pieces

2 tablespoons to ¼ cup Sichuan whole peppercorns

15 to 30 Sichuan facing heaven chiles

1 cup Chinese cooking wine

½ cup light soy sauce

18 cups cold water or All-Purpose Simple Chicken Broth (page 32)

4 bay leaves

Salt

Ground white pepper

1. In a large stockpot, heat the oil and hot bean sauce on medium-high for 30 seconds.

2. Carefully add the garlic, scallions, Sichuan peppercorns, and chiles. Cook for 1 to 2 minutes, being careful not to burn the ingredients. Slowly add the wine and soy sauce and stir for another minute.

3. Carefully add the water and bay leaves to the pot and bring to a boil. Simmer for 30 minutes.

4. Remove the bay leaves. Season to taste with salt and ground pepper. Serve with the aromatics.

5. Refrigerate the broth in an airtight container for up to 5 days or freeze for up to 3 months.

PAIRING TIP: Make sure you have an icy-cold beverage nearby—you will need it!

SPICY AND HERBAL LAMB BROTH

CHINESE, MEAT, MONGOLIAN, SPICY
MAKES 20 CUPS | PREP TIME: 20 minutes | COOK TIME: 2 hours 15 minutes

Rich and savory, this is a bold, complex broth giving a nod to its origin in Mongolia. Inspired by the renowned Mongolian hot-pot chain Little Sheep Hot Pot, many herbs and spices go into developing the broth's aromatic and layered flavors that complement the strong-tasting flavor of the lamb bones used to make it. Mutton is what is typically used in Asia. If lamb bones are hard to find, you can substitute with chicken bones. If you have a split pot, this is a popular broth base to offer both spicy and non-spicy versions. Make the entire broth recipe and remove half to cook with ingredients noted in the variation tip below.

30 cups cold water, divided

4 pounds lamb or mutton bones (ask the butcher counter for this)

5 peeled (1½-inch-wide-by-¼-inch-thick) ginger slices, divided

5 scallions, both white and green parts, cut into 3-inch pieces, divided

12 whole black peppercorns

½ cup light soy sauce

15 garlic cloves, peeled and smashed

15 whole cloves

10 dried Chinese red dates

1. Fill a large stockpot with 10 cups of water and bring to a boil. Add the lamb bones to the water.

2. Add 2 slices of ginger and cook for 5 minutes to blanch the bones to remove impurities.

3. Drain and rinse the bones thoroughly with cold water.

4. Rinse and wipe the stockpot then fill it with the remaining 20 cups of water. Add the lamb bones, the remaining 3 slices of ginger, the white parts of the scallions, and the peppercorns. Bring to a boil, partially covered, then simmer over low heat for 1½ to 2 hours.

5. Skim off any scum that floats to the surface. Remove and discard the bones and strain the liquid through a sieve.

continued ››

5 star anise

5 dried bay leaves

2 (3-inch) cinnamon sticks

2 tablespoons dried
  goji berries

Ground white pepper

6. Return the broth to the stockpot. Add the soy sauce, garlic, cloves, dates, star anise, bay leaves, cinnamon sticks, goji berries, and pepper. Bring the broth to a boil over high heat; cover, lower the heat to low, and simmer until fragrant for 15 minutes, leaving the aromatics in.

7. Refrigerate the broth in an airtight container for up to 5 days or freeze for up to 3 months.

SUBSTITUTION: You can use 20 cups of All-Purpose Simple Chicken Broth (page 32) in place of the lamb broth and skip to step 6.

VARIATION: To make a half batch of a spicy version, in a separate medium pot over medium heat, add ¼ to ½ cup of oil. When hot, cook 10 to 20 Sichuan facing heaven chiles and ½ to 2 teaspoons of red pepper flakes for 1 to 2 minutes, being careful not to burn the ingredients. Carefully pour in half of the broth (10 cups) with aromatics; simmer for 10 minutes and serve in a split pot. Or double these ingredients to make the entire broth spicy.

EASY SMOKY *SHACHA* BARBECUE BROTH

45 MINUTES OR LESS, CHINESE, SEAFOOD, SPICY, TAIWANESE
MAKES 20 CUPS | PREP TIME: 5 minutes | COOK TIME: 10 minutes

A Taiwanese-inspired favorite, *shacha* (or *sa cha*) sauce's robust grill flavors are easily enjoyed as a hot-pot broth prepared with just plain water or chicken. Soybean oil, garlic, chiles, brill fish, and dried shrimp make up its savory, smoky barbecue profile and slight spiciness.

18 cups cold water or All-Purpose Simple Chicken Broth (page 32)

1 cup *shacha* or *sa cha* barbecue sauce

¾ to 1 cup fish sauce

2 tablespoons granulated sugar

¼ cup light soy sauce

1. In a large stockpot, bring the water to a boil.

2. Mix the *shacha* sauce well to combine the oil and solids. Add the *shacha* sauce, fish sauce, sugar, and soy sauce to the pot. Stir well. Turn the heat to low and simmer for 10 minutes.

3. Refrigerate the broth in an airtight container for up to 5 days. Not recommended for freezing.

VARIATION: To add tang to the broth, gradually add up to 1 cup of unseasoned rice vinegar or white vinegar to taste.

INGREDIENT TIP: *Shacha* is one of those tricky condiments to find, as it is not always indicated on the label. Look for Bullhead, the most popular brand (with a cartoon bull on the front), also offered in a vegetarian option. Lee Kum Kee has their product clearly labeled as Sa Cha Sauce; however, many brands just call it barbecue sauce or satay sauce. Read the ingredient label to verify that this is indeed the right condiment. If it contains peanuts, then it is a different kind of satay sauce used for Southeast Asian cooking.

SOYBEAN OR MISO BROTH

JAPANESE, KOREAN, MEATLESS
MAKES 20 CUPS | PREP TIME: 4 hours (for soaking) | COOK TIME: 15 minutes

A healthy, flavorful broth can be simply made with fermented soybean paste from Korea's *doenjang* or miso from Japan. Soaking the kombu, or kelp, a nutrient-rich seaweed, extracts the umami flavor, coming off as a slimy substance. You can simmer the kombu in the broth for a few minutes, but it should never be boiled, or it will become bitter. If you prefer to use miso for a more Japanese profile, omit the garlic. The lighter the color of miso, the sweeter and milder the flavor. For hot pot, I recommend a red soybean–based miso that has a deep umami flavor.

12 dried medium shiitake mushrooms

2 cups warm water

4 pieces kombu, each about 2 by 6 inches

18 cups cold water

3 tablespoons neutral cooking oil

4 scallions, both white and green parts, cut into 3-inch pieces

2 medium onions, sliced

12 to 15 garlic cloves, coarsely chopped (optional)

1 cup Korean *doenjang* or Japanese miso

Salt

1. In a medium bowl, soak the mushrooms in the warm water for 4 hours. Remove the mushrooms from the water, discard the stems, and thinly slice the caps. Reserve the water, straining out any debris.

2. Wipe the kombu with a damp cloth to clean the cloudy residue on its surface. With scissors, cut into 2-inch pieces. In a large stockpot, soak the kombu in the cold water for 2 hours. Remove the kelp.

3. In a large stockpot, heat the oil over medium-high, add the scallions, onions, and mushrooms; sauté for 2 minutes until fragrant and the onions are soft.

4. Pour in the kelp stock and reserved mushroom liquid. Bring to a boil and add the garlic (if using). Let cook for 1 minute and add the *doenjang* paste.

5. Cover and simmer for 15 minutes. Adjust the seasonings and salt to taste. No need to strain the ingredients.

6. Refrigerate the broth in an airtight container for 2 to 3 days or freeze for up to 3 months.

DASHI BROTH

GLUTEN-FREE, JAPANESE, SEAFOOD
MAKES 20 CUPS | PREP TIME: 2 hours (for soaking) | COOK TIME: 10 minutes

A light clear broth composed of dashi (kombu and bonito flakes) is the hallmark of Japanese cuisine and the starter base of a good miso soup. Bonito flakes are the shavings from skipjack tuna that has been simmered, smoked, and fermented. I also have included a variation using dried anchovies or sardines. Called *iriko* or *niboshi* dashi, this is a very common broth choice because these tiny fish are more affordable than kombu or *katsuobushi*. It makes a lovely briny fish broth.

4 (2-by-6-inch) pieces kombu (kelp)

20 cups cold water

4 cups dried bonito flakes (*katsuobushi*)

1. Using a damp cloth, wipe the kombu to clean the cloudy residue on its surface.

2. Fill a large stockpot with the water, then add the seaweed and soak for at least 2 hours. You can heat and simmer the kombu for a few minutes to optimize the flavor, but it should never be boiled, as it will turn your broth slimy and bitter. Remove the kelp.

3. Bring the liquid to a boil and add the bonito flakes. Turn down the heat to simmer for a few minutes while removing foam on top thoroughly. Turn off the heat. Allow the bonito to sink to the pot bottom.

4. Strain the liquid through a sieve into another pot (do not squeeze liquid from the remaining dried bonito flakes, as it will impart bitterness).

5. Refrigerate the broth in an airtight container for 2 to 3 days or freeze for up to 3 months.

SUBSTITUTION: If you are in a hurry, instant dashi stock sold in granules is a good alternative.

VARIATION: To make Japanese *iriko* or *niboshi* dashi, use 2 cups dried anchovies or sardines (packages found in Asian grocery stores) and 20 cups of water. Prepare the dried fish by removing the heads and guts around the belly area (bottom side), to prevent bitterness in the broth. It is black and easy to pull out.

In a large stockpot, soak the fish in water for at least 30 minutes or up to overnight. Bring the water to a boil, then lower the heat to low and cook for 8 to 10 minutes. Strain the clear liquid through a sieve into another large pot.

MILKY WHITE FISH BROTH

CHINESE, GLUTEN-FREE, SEAFOOD
MAKES 20 CUPS | PREP TIME: 10 minutes | COOK TIME: 45 minutes

My mom showed me this technique for white broth—it's like an ancient Chinese secret! Fish broth is prepared by first sautéing fish heads or bones in a little oil until golden with ginger slices to remove any fishy aroma. Then boiling water is poured onto the fish in the stockpot to release the flavors, turning the water white. It will develop into a milky white broth as it simmers. To make the recipe more practical I have called for smelts, which are inexpensive, accessible, and great in achieving a lovely, slightly sweet milky fish broth.

¼ cup neutral cooking oil

4 peeled (1½-inch-wide and ¼-inch-thick) ginger slices, divided

3 to 4 pounds whole smelt (or look for fish heads and bones from a white fish such as carp or threadfin at the fish counter in an Asian supermarket)

20 cups boiling hot water, divided

1. In a large stockpot, heat the oil over medium heat. Add 2 slices of ginger and let cook for 30 seconds.

2. Add the smelt. Sauté the fish until golden on both sides. Be careful not to burn, or the broth will be dark and contain charred bits. Remove the ginger slices.

3. Turn the heat to medium-high. Carefully pour 10 cups of boiling hot water over the fish. Once the water hits the pot, it will bubble vigorously; this is when the broth will turn white. Add the remaining 10 cups of water and 2 ginger slices.

4. Lower the heat to medium and simmer, partially covered, for 45 minutes, skimming off any scum and extra oil that floats to the surface. Strain the liquid through a sieve into another pot.

5. Refrigerate the broth in an airtight container for 2 days or freeze for up to 3 months.

TANGY AND SWEET BROTH
(BÒ NHÚNG DẤM)

45 MINUTES OR LESS, GLUTEN-FREE, MEATLESS, VIETNAMESE
MAKES 16 CUPS | PREP TIME: 5 minutes | COOK TIME: 15 minutes

Bò nhúng dấm translates to "beef vinegar dip," but it can certainly be used to cook veggies! The dining experience with this broth is likened to Japanese sukiyaki, in that you cook ingredients in liquid meant to flavor the ingredients, not enjoyed like a soup. This tangy and sweet profile is the go-to hot pot my husband's Vietnamese family makes to enjoy with beef. It's simply water (variations can include fresh coconut juice or even beer), rice vinegar, sugar, salt, and some aromatics. My father-in-law liked to use 7UP instead of sugar, and it was always a hit!

8 cups cold water

4 cups unseasoned rice vinegar or white vinegar

3 (12-ounce) cans 7UP or Sprite soda

2 tablespoons salt

2 large onions, halved

6 celery stalks, cut into 3 pieces

1. In a large stockpot, combine the water, vinegar, soda, and salt over medium-high heat and bring to a boil.

2. Add the onions and celery. Simmer, partially covered, for 15 minutes.

3. Serve immediately.

INGREDIENT TIP: This broth is not meant as a soup but as a flavoring to ingredients. Use 12 cups to start the hot pot, and the other 4 cups for replenishing.

SAVORY PHO BEEF BROTH

GLUTEN-FREE, MEAT, VIETNAMESE
MAKES 20 CUPS | PREP TIME: 45 minutes | COOK TIME: 3 hours

This is my authentic broth recipe to make pho beef noodle soup. I used to think it cooked for half a day, but it is far easier and less time-consuming. I like the bones with a little marrow for added collagen and body in the broth. The extra steps in toasting your spices and broiling the onions and ginger make a huge difference in the final broth flavor, which is full of distinct warm spices and savory characteristics.

33 cups cold water, divided

4 pounds beef bones (beef leg, shins, knuckles, and knees; with some marrow is best)

2 peeled (1½-inch-wide and ¼-inch-thick) ginger slices

1 large white onion, unpeeled and halved

3-inch piece fresh ginger, halved lengthwise

Neutral cooking oil, for brushing

4 star anise

4 whole cloves

2 (3-inch) cinnamon sticks

2 brown cardamom pods, bruised (optional)

1. Fill a large stockpot with 12 cups of water and bring to a boil. Place the beef bones into the water.

2. Add the slices of ginger and cook for 5 minutes to blanch the bones and remove impurities.

3. Drain and rinse the bones thoroughly with cold water.

4. Rinse and wipe the stockpot. Fill with the remaining 21 cups of water, add the beef bones, and bring to a boil.

5. Meanwhile, preheat the broiler to high and place the baking rack 6 to 8 inches away from the heating element.

6. On a baking sheet, place the onion and ginger halves cut-side up, and brush with a bit of oil. Broil for 15 to 20 minutes, until the tops of the onion and ginger are nicely charred. Remove and set aside.

continued ››

1 (6-ounce) daikon,
  roughly chopped

⅓ cup fish sauce

¼ cup golden or
  granulated sugar

2 tablespoons sea salt

7. In a pan, toast the star anise, cloves, cinnamon, and cardamom pods over medium-high heat for about 3 minutes, stirring, until fragrant. Place the smaller aromatics in a spice ball or wrap them in a cheese cloth. Add the spices and cinnamon sticks to the pot. Add the charred onion, ginger, and daikon.

8. Bring the water back to a boil over high heat. Lower the heat to medium-low; simmer for 2½ hours, frequently skimming the surface of scum and oil.

9. Stir in the fish sauce, sugar, and salt and return to a boil, then simmer over low heat for 30 minutes. Taste and season the broth as needed. Strain the broth through a strainer into another large pot.

10. Refrigerate the broth in an airtight container for 3 days or freeze for up to 3 months.

HOT-AND-SOUR TOM YUM BROTH

45 MINUTES OR LESS, GLUTEN-FREE, MEATLESS, THAI

MAKES 20 CUPS | PREP TIME: 10 minutes | COOK TIME: 20 minutes

Tom yum is a spicy, savory, and tangy brew. Galangal, a ginger-like rhizome, adds a distinctive lemony flavor, and lime leaves impart a wonderful citrus fragrance. Sweet and spicy Thai chile paste consists of roasted aromatics and shrimp paste. Instead, I mix equal parts *shacha* barbecue sauce with sambal oelek to achieve a similar flavor. If you don't have these, add chopped fresh red chiles instead.

3 tablespoons neutral cooking oil

2 (2-inch) pieces fresh galangal root or ginger root, thinly sliced

3 to 4 lemongrass stalks, outer layers removed, crushed and cut into 4-inch pieces, or ½ cup chopped lemongrass, frozen and thawed

20 cups cold water

½ to ¾ cup fish sauce

2 to 4 tablespoons Thai chile paste (*nam prik pao*) or chopped red chiles

2 (1.41-ounce) packets tamarind soup mix

10 lime leaves, torn

2 tablespoons granulated sugar

½ cup freshly squeezed lime juice

1. In a large stockpot, heat the oil over medium-high heat. Add the galangal and lemongrass. Cook for 1 minute, stirring until fragrant.

2. Add the water, fish sauce, chile paste, tamarind soup mix, lime leaves, and sugar. Bring to a boil.

3. Lower the heat to medium-low and simmer for 15 minutes.

4. Strain the broth through a strainer into another large pot. Stir in the lime juice before serving.

5. Refrigerate the broth in an airtight container for 5 days or freeze for up to 3 months.

SUBSTITUTION: Use 10 (1-inch) thinly sliced peels from two limes instead of lime leaves.

VARIATION: Omit the sugar and add 1 cup of fresh or canned pineapple chunks.

CREAMY COCONUT BROTH

45 MINUTES OR LESS, CAMBODIAN, GLUTEN-FREE, MALAYSIAN, THAI

MAKES 20 CUPS | PREP TIME: **10 minutes** | COOK TIME: **10 minutes**

Popularly used in Cambodian hot pot, this creamy broth is called *ya-hon*. Creaminess is key to imparting that richness to ingredients cooked in it. I've called for full-fat coconut milk not the coconut milk thinned for drinking. The more *shacha* sauce you add, the spicier it will be, and it will give an orange slick to the creamy broth. The rich texture and flavors make a delicious broth to build on other coconut-based Southeast Asian hot pots by adding seasonings like curry powder, Thai curry paste, and aromatics.

4 (13.5-ounce) cans full-fat coconut milk

1 to 2 cups *shacha* or *sa cha* barbecue sauce (Bullhead brand or Vegetarian label)

8 cups coconut water or coconut soda (Coco Rico is a popular brand)

4 cups cold water or All-Purpose Simple Chicken Broth (page 32)

⅓ cup fish sauce

2 teaspoons salt

¾ cup crushed roasted peanuts (optional)

1. In a large stockpot, bring the coconut milk to a simmer over medium heat, stirring often to prevent burning.

2. Mix the *shacha* sauce well to combine the oil and solids and stir into the coconut milk to combine and dissolve.

3. Then add the coconut water and cold water. Stir to combine and bring to a light boil over medium-high heat.

4. Add the fish sauce and salt, adjusting to your taste. Lower the heat and simmer for 5 minutes.

5. Finish with the peanuts (if using) or add to your dipping sauce.

6. Refrigerate the broth in an airtight container for 3 days.

VARIATION: *Shacha* sauce is prepared with seafood. If you prefer, buy the vegetarian version to make your broth and substitute soy sauce instead of fish sauce.

BOK CHOY, SHIITAKE, AND CHIVE DUMPLINGS, PAGE 60

CHAPTER FOUR

Sauces and Homemade Ingredients

SAVORY SOY DIPPING SAUCE

45 MINUTES OR LESS, ALL-PURPOSE, EASY, MEATLESS
MAKES 1 CUP | PREP TIME: 5 minutes

Soy sauce is a popular base to build your dipping sauce. I use a naturally brewed light soy sauce. It is lighter in color, thinner, and saltier than regular soy sauce. Light is soy sauce's first press, likened to extra-virgin olive oil, where you get the purest flavor. Feel free to substitute the soy sauce you prefer. These sauce variations work with all hot pot-styles.

FOR SAVORY SOY DIPPING SAUCE

1 cup light soy sauce

2 tablespoons sliced scallions, both white and green parts

1 tablespoon sesame oil or spicy oil

1 tablespoon chopped fresh cilantro

1 to 2 garlic cloves, minced

Dashes ground white pepper

**FOR TANGY SOY DIPPING SAUCE
(MAKES ABOUT 1¼ CUPS)**

½ cup light soy sauce

½ cup rice vinegar

2 tablespoons sesame oil

1 tablespoon freshly squeezed lemon juice

½ teaspoon toasted sesame seeds

Red pepper chile flakes (optional)

FOR PIQUANT SOY DIPPING SAUCE

1 cup light soy sauce

1 tablespoon prepared wasabi, hot mustard, or Dijon mustard

To make the dipping sauces: In small bowls, mix all the ingredients for each sauce. Serve in individual bowls for dipping. Refrigerate in an airtight container for up to 3 days.

INGREDIENT TIP: Lao Gan Ma's Chili Crisp is a chunky, spicy oil touted in *New York Times Magazine* as a must-have condiment even for ice cream! It contains oil, chiles, onion, black beans, Sichuan peppercorns, and seasonings and is a perfect spicy oil to use in the Savory Soy Dipping Sauce.

AROMATIC SCALLION AND GINGER OIL

45 MINUTES OR LESS, ALL-PURPOSE, CHINESE, EASY, MEATLESS

MAKES ½ CUP | PREP TIME: 5 minutes | COOK TIME: 2 minutes

This is a classic Chinese oil best served alongside poached or steamed chicken. It also goes well with fish. Enliven your hot pot dipping sauce with a spoonful of this aromatic oil that will be sure to please.

4 scallions, both white and green parts, finely chopped

1½-inch knob ginger, peeled and minced

Dash salt

Dash ground white pepper

⅓ cup neutral cooking oil

1. In a small bowl, combine the scallions, ginger, salt, and pepper.

2. In a small pot, heat the oil over high heat until smoking and carefully pour over the onion mixture. The oil will sizzle as it slightly cooks the ingredients.

3. Refrigerate in an airtight container for up to 3 days.

VARIATION: Make this without ginger for aromatic scallion oil.

SILKY EGG AND *SHACHA* BARBECUE SAUCE

45 MINUTES OR LESS, ALL-PURPOSE, CHINESE, EASY, TAIWANESE

MAKES ½ CUP | PREP TIME: 5 minutes | COOK TIME: 2 minutes

This is a Taiwanese dipping-sauce favorite with *shacha*'s robust grilled smoky flavors and tastes delicious mixed with a raw egg. It partners well with beef and other seafood. The raw egg tempers the heat and adds silkiness to the foods dipped in it. The U.S. Food and Drug Administration recommends using pasteurized eggs. Because this contains raw egg, it is best to make it right before serving.

¼ cup *shacha* or *sa cha* barbecue sauce (Bullhead brand or Vegetarian label)

¼ cup light soy sauce

1 to 2 garlic cloves, minced (optional)

4 large eggs (pasteurized)

1. Mix the oil and solids of the *shacha* sauce to combine into a paste.

2. In a bowl, combine the *shacha*, soy sauce, and garlic (if using). Mix well.

3. Divide the sauce into four dipping bowls. When ready to serve, crack 1 egg in each and mix to combine.

CREAMY SESAME DIPPING SAUCE

45 MINUTES OR LESS, ALL-PURPOSE, EASY, MEATLESS
MAKES ABOUT 1 CUP | PREP TIME: 5 minutes

The nutty creaminess from sesame paste adds body and delicious flavor in combination with savory soy sauce and tangy rice vinegar. If you have black vinegar, a fermented sweet and tangy vinegar from China's Chinkiang, it is a wonderful complement to soy sauce and sesame. You can also use rice vinegar in its place. This is an ideal dip for lamb and beef and Japanese shabu-shabu.

⅓ cup tahini sesame paste or prepared Chinese sesame paste

3 tablespoons light soy sauce

2 tablespoons rice vinegar or Chinkiang black vinegar

2 tablespoons to ¼ cup cold water

1 teaspoon granulated sugar

Few dashes ground white pepper

1 tablespoon sesame oil

Chile oil, for finishing

Toasted sesame seeds, for garnish

1. In a bowl, combine the sesame paste, soy sauce, vinegar, and 2 tablespoons of water. Mix well until blended, adding 1 tablespoon more of water at a time to get the right consistency.

2. Add the sugar and pepper. Finish with sesame oil, chile oil, and sesame seeds.

3. Refrigerate in an airtight container for up to 3 days.

SUBSTITUTION: Use peanut butter instead of sesame paste.

VARIATION: Add chopped garlic, scallions, and cilantro for even more flavor.

SWEET AND SOUR CHILE SAUCE

45 MINUTES OR LESS, EASY, MEATLESS, SPICY
MAKES ABOUT 1¾ CUPS | PREP TIME: 5 minutes | COOK TIME: 5 minutes

This is a well-balanced sweet, sour, and spicy dipping sauce that lends ingredients another flavor dimension and gives them a glazed texture. Feel free to omit the chiles if you want it non-spicy.

½ cup ketchup

½ cup white or rice vinegar

⅓ to ½ cup granulated sugar

2 teaspoons light soy sauce

2 teaspoons neutral cooking oil

1 to 2 garlic cloves, minced

1 to 2 red chiles, seeded and sliced

3 tablespoons cold water

2 tablespoons cornstarch

1. In a small bowl, combine the ketchup, vinegar, sugar, and soy sauce and whisk well.

2. In a saucepan, heat the oil, garlic, and chiles over medium heat and let sizzle for 20 seconds.

3. Stir in the sauce mixture and bring to a low boil.

4. In a small bowl, blend the water and cornstarch and stir into the sauce. Simmer for 1 minute, or until thickened. Let cool before serving.

5. Refrigerate in an airtight container for up to 3 days.

VARIATION: Reduce the sugar to ¼ cup and add 1 cup of fresh or canned (well-drained) crushed pineapple, sautéed for 30 seconds with the sauce before adding the cornstarch mixture.

SEASONED FISH SAUCE
(NUOC MAM CHAM)

45 MINUTES OR LESS, EASY, SEAFOOD, THAI, VIETNAMESE

MAKES ABOUT ¾ CUP | PREP TIME: 5 minutes

Pure fish sauce, known as *nuoc mam* in Vietnam, *nam pla* in Thailand, or simply as liquid gold, is made from salted fermented fish and has a very pungent salty flavor. This is the soy sauce equivalent in Southeast Asian cuisines. Seasoned with sugar and vinegar or lime juice, it captures the region's classic flavor combination of sweet, salty, and sour. My Vietnamese family-in-law serves it as a dip for lettuce leaves wrapped in hot-pot ingredients cooked in Tangy and Sweet Broth (*Bò Nhúng Dấm*; page 102).

¼ cup granulated sugar

⅓ cup boiling water

2 tablespoons fish sauce (I like both Squid and Three Crabs brands)

2 tablespoons white vinegar or freshly squeezed lime juice

1 to 2 garlic cloves, minced

Sambal oelek or chopped red chiles

1. In a small bowl, dissolve the sugar in the boiling water.

2. Mix in the fish sauce and vinegar and leave to cool.

3. Add the garlic and season with sambal oelek to taste.

4. Refrigerate in an airtight container for up to 3 days.

SIMPLE SUKIYAKI SAUCE (*WARISHITA*)

45 MINUTES OR LESS, EASY, JAPANESE, MEATLESS
MAKES 2 CUPS | PREP TIME: 5 minutes

This light sauce, *warishita*, is used for sukiyaki hot pot. Its primary ingredient is mirin, which is a sweet cooking wine and an essential Japanese condiment. The name *suki-yaki* has taken a myriad of styles in Asia. In Laos, hot pot is also called *sukiyaki* and in Thailand *suki*, but the flavoring is different, and the broth is meant to be sipped. In Japan, this sweet and savory sauce is intended to flavor the ingredients quickly cooked in it, but it is not used like a soup broth.

1 cup mirin

½ cup light soy sauce or Japanese shoyu

⅓ cup water

2 tablespoons Japanese cooking sake or Chinese cooking wine

2 tablespoons granulated sugar

1. In a medium saucepan, combine the mirin, soy sauce, water, sake, and sugar and bring to a boil over medium-high heat. Reduce the heat to low and simmer for about 5 minutes, stirring occasionally. Remove from the heat and let cool before serving.

2. Refrigerate in an airtight container for up to 5 days or freeze for up to a month.

SUBSTITUTION: Instead of mirin, use 1 cup of Chinese cooking wine or rice vinegar with 5 tablespoons of sugar added.

PORK AND SHRIMP WONTONS

ALL-PURPOSE, CHINESE, MEAT, SEAFOOD
MAKES 70 WONTONS | PREP TIME: 1 hour | COOK TIME: 3 to 4 minutes

Wonton varieties are easy to find in Asian supermarkets. If you can't find them or want to try making your own, I am happy to share this recipe I grew up cooking with my family. The recipe makes a lot of wontons, so serve up some to eat right away and freeze the remainder (see page 61 for freezing instructions). You can find wonton wrappers in an Asian supermarket in the refrigerated aisle.

1 pound lean ground pork, chicken, or turkey

2 tablespoons water

1 tablespoon Chinese cooking wine or dry sherry (optional)

2 teaspoons chicken broth mix powder

2 teaspoons light soy sauce

1 teaspoon salt

½ teaspoon sesame oil

⅛ teaspoon ground white pepper

14 ounces shrimp, shelled, cleaned, rinsed, and finely chopped

1 tablespoon cornstarch

1 (7.5-ounce) package wonton wrappers (about 70)

1. In a large bowl, combine the pork and water and mix with a fork for about 2 minutes (for a smoother texture).

2. Add the cooking wine (if using), broth powder, soy sauce, salt, sesame oil, and pepper. Stir in the shrimp to incorporate. Mix in the cornstarch and stir until fully combined.

3. Cover and refrigerate for at least 1 hour for the flavors to blend.

4. Place a little less than 1 tablespoon of filling in the center of a wonton wrapper. Moisten the edges of the wrapper with a bit of water, gather up the sides to encase the filling in a ball, and pinch and twist the top to seal. Repeat with the remaining wrappers and filling.

5. Cook immediately (for about 4 minutes for frozen and 3 minutes for fresh—they are ready when they float to the surface) or freeze. Do not refrigerate or they will get moist and stick to the plate.

BASIC DUMPLING DOUGH (FOR SOUPS)

45 MINUTES OR LESS, EASY, GLUTEN-FREE, MEATLESS,
MAKES 24 (3-INCH) WRAPPERS | PREP TIME: 30 minutes

Dumplings are a highlight in enjoying hot pot. If you want to try making your own, it is best to make your own dumpling wrappers, too. Convenient store-bought dumpling wrappers are best for steaming or panfrying. For boiling, thin wonton wrappers are typically used. Dumplings for soups, such as the ones made in this recipe, are opaque and cook up thicker with a nice chewy texture. While many dough recipes require at least 30 minutes to rest, this one can be rolled right away.

1 cup all-purpose flour
½ teaspoon salt
⅓ cup boiling water

1. In a medium bowl, mix the flour and salt with a wooden spoon. Slowly pour in the boiling water while stirring. The mixture will turn into dry dough pieces.

2. Dust a flat surface with flour. Using your hand, gather the dough and knead for about 5 minutes, until smooth. Roll into a 1-inch log, then cut in half. Place the logs side by side and cut into half again. Place the four pieces side by side and cut each into six pieces.

3. Using a rolling pin (a small one works best), roll each dough piece into a 3-inch-wide round. Dust a little flour in between wrappers to prevent sticking. You can make this ahead overnight, and store wrapped with plastic.

BOK CHOY, SHIITAKE, AND CHIVE DUMPLINGS

ALL-PURPOSE, CHINESE, MEATLESS
MAKES 24 DUMPLINGS | PREP TIME: 1 hour, plus 4 hours for soaking
COOK TIME: 3 to 5 minutes

Vegetable dumplings are always lovely with hot pot. For soup, ones in the market are usually Korean style, filled with kimchi, chives, napa cabbage, and sometimes sweet potato noodles. This recipe is Chinese inspired with my favorite three vegetable ingredients, which match deliciously with my homemade chewy dumpling wrapper. If I will be stir-frying the mushrooms, I like to add a bit of sugar to the mushroom-soaking liquid to impart sweetness for a deeper flavor.

6 medium dried whole shiitake mushrooms

1 cup warm water

½ teaspoon granulated sugar

1 tablespoon neutral cooking oil

1 to 2 garlic cloves, minced

1 handful Asian chives, finely chopped, or scallions, green parts only

5 baby bok choy, finely chopped

1 teaspoon light soy sauce

Salt

Ground white pepper

1 teaspoon cornstarch

1. In a small bowl, soak the shiitake mushrooms in the warm water mixed with the sugar for 4 hours. Remove the mushrooms from the soaking water, reserving the water and straining out any debris. Rinse the mushroom gills of any dirt and squeeze well. Discard the stems and finely chop the mushrooms.

2. In a skillet, heat the oil over medium-high heat and stir-fry the mushrooms and garlic for 1 minute, until fragrant. Add the chives, then bok choy and stir-fry for about 1 minute. Season with 1 tablespoon of mushroom-soaking liquid, the soy sauce, salt, and pepper. Scatter the cornstarch and mix well to firm up. Let cool completely for about 15 minutes.

continued ››

24 Basic Dumpling Dough (page 59) wrappers or store-bought dumpling wrappers

3. Assemble the dumplings right before cooking. Place 1 tablespoon of filling in the center of a wrapper. Wet half the wrapper rim with water, then fold the wrapper over so that the dry edge meets the wet one. Press or pleat along the seam to seal tightly. Repeat to make all the dumplings.

4. Cook immediately (for about 4 minutes for frozen and 3 minutes for fresh—they are ready when they float to the surface) or freeze. Do not refrigerate, or they will get moist and stick together and to the plate.

PREP TIP: To freeze, lay the dumplings on a baking sheet and freeze for 1 hour to prevent sticking. Place plastic wrap on the bottom of a container. Lay the uncooked dumplings in a single layer, then cover with plastic wrap to add a second layer. Repeat with a final layer of wrap over the top before sealing with a lid. Freeze for up to 2 months.

MEAT AND VEGETABLE DUMPLINGS

ALL-PURPOSE, CHINESE, MEAT

MAKES 24 DUMPLINGS | PREP TIME: 1 hour | COOK TIME: 3 to 5 minutes

Pork-and-chive is the most popular Chinese dumpling filling. However, in this recipe you can interchange another white meat such as chicken or turkey and use leeks or napa cabbage if you prefer a mellow accompaniment, as chives have a strong flavor. You can always tell when dumplings are cooked—they float to the surface.

8 ounces lean ground meat (pork, chicken, or turkey)

1 tablespoon water

½ cup finely chopped Asian chives, leeks (white parts only), or napa cabbage (¼ small cabbage, leaves blanched, squeezed dry)

2 teaspoons light soy sauce

½ teaspoon salt

2 dashes ground white pepper

1 teaspoon sesame oil

1 teaspoon cornstarch

24 Basic Dumpling Dough (page 59) wrappers or store-bought dumpling wrappers

1. In a medium bowl, combine the meat and water. Mix with a fork for about 2 minutes (for a smoother meat texture). Add the chives, soy sauce, salt, and pepper; then add the oil and cornstarch. Incorporate well.

2. Cover and refrigerate for at least 1 hour for the flavors to blend.

3. Assemble the dumplings right before cooking. Place 1 tablespoon of filling in the center of a wrapper. Wet half the wrapper rim with water, then fold the wrapper over so that the dry edge meets the wet one. Press or pleat along the seam to seal tightly. Repeat to make all the dumplings.

4. Cook immediately (for about 4 minutes for frozen and 3 minutes for fresh—they are ready when they float to the surface) or freeze (see page 61). Do not refrigerate or they will get moist and stick together and to the plate.

SICHUAN SPICY *MA LA* MARINATED FISH

45 MINUTES OR LESS, CHINESE, EASY, GLUTEN-FREE, SEAFOOD, SPICY

SERVES 4 TO 6 | PREP TIME: 30 minutes | COOK TIME: 1 to 2 minutes

The wonder of this popular casserole dish of white fish submerged in *ma la tang* (soup) is how delicate the flesh remains; not overly spicy despite being bathed in the oily sea of red hot chiles and scattered with tongue-numbing peppercorns. The best fish to use are mild-tasting white ones with lean flesh. Because they are delicate, it is best to cook them in a ladle basket. If you like to serve this in the Spicy and Tingly *Ma La* Broth (page 35), use the non-spicy fish marinade recipe. Or give it the complete spicy treatment and serve cooked in milder broths.

FOR SPICY FISH MARINADE

1 tablespoon neutral cooking oil

1 tablespoon Sichuan hot bean sauce (*doubanjiang* or Chinese chile bean paste)

4 garlic cloves, coarsely chopped

½ tablespoon Sichuan peppercorns

1 egg white, egg yolk reserved (if pasteurized, add to your dipping sauce)

Salt

Ground white pepper

2 teaspoons Chinese cooking wine

1 tablespoon cornstarch

1 pound white firm basa fish fillet (or cod, snapper, sole), cut into 2 bite-size pieces

FOR FISH MARINADE

1 egg white, egg yolk reserved (if pasteurized, add to your dipping sauce)

Salt

Ground white pepper

2 teaspoons Chinese cooking wine

1 tablespoon cornstarch

1. To make either marinade: In a medium bowl, mix all the ingredients of your marinade choice; toss well with the fish pieces. Set aside to marinate for 20 minutes to 1 hour in the refrigerator.

2. Remove the peppercorns from the fish before cooking.

HOMEMADE MEATBALLS

45 MINUTES OR LESS, ALL-PURPOSE, EASY
MAKES ABOUT 20 MEATBALLS | PREP TIME: 20 minutes | COOK TIME: 3 minutes

All kinds of meatballs and seafood balls are available at Asian supermarkets to choose from for your favorite hot pot; however, if for some reason they are difficult to find or you want to try your hand at making them yourself, they are really a cinch to do. The key is their characteristic springiness. The longer you stir, the bouncier and lighter the texture. For a heat kick, try the delicious spicy variation with ground chile and cumin.

1 pound lean ground meat (pork, chicken, turkey, beef, or lamb)

2 tablespoons cold water

2 teaspoons light soy sauce

2 teaspoons sesame oil

2 teaspoons cornstarch

½ teaspoon granulated garlic salt or regular salt

½ teaspoon ground white pepper

1. In a medium bowl, combine the meat and water. Using a fork or a pair of chopsticks, rake the meat back and forth while turning the bowl for about 5 minutes until sticky (this gives the meatballs a smooth, springy texture).

2. Add the soy sauce, sesame oil, cornstarch, garlic salt, and pepper and continue to mix for 2 minutes more.

3. The traditional Chinese way to shape meatballs is to grab a small handful of the meatball paste. Squeeze the mixture into a ball by tightening your fist; the paste will come out through the "hole" made by your thumb and forefinger (about 1½ tablespoons). Use a teaspoon in your other hand to scoop and shape the ball. Place onto a plate. Repeat with the remaining meat mixture. Alternatively, you could roll the paste between wet palms to shape the meatballs.

4. Cover and refrigerate for up to overnight before serving or freeze for up to 2 months.

VARIATION: To make a spicy version, add 1 to 1½ teaspoons each of ground chile pepper and ground cumin to the meat mixture (works best with beef or lamb). Test one meatball by cooking in boiling water and adjust the seasoning if required.

PREP TIP: To freeze, lay the meatballs on a baking sheet and freeze for 1 hour to prevent sticking. Place them in a container or reusable plastic bag. Freeze for up to 2 months.

TOM YUM VEGETABLE HOT POT, PAGE 82

CHAPTER FIVE

Vegetable and Tofu Hot Pots

MARVELOUS MUSHROOM HOT POT

45 MINUTES OR LESS, CHINESE, MEATLESS, SPICY
SERVES 4 | PREP TIME: 15 minutes | COOK TIME: 15 minutes

Mushroom lovers, this is the hot pot for you! It's inspired by Yunnan, China's south-west mountainous region, home to a vast diversity of wild mushrooms (90 percent of China's mushrooms grow here). With a fragrant, earthy mixed mushroom broth, it is best enjoyed with a variety of mushrooms to further develop its rich umami flavors. Serve with wheat gluten and noodles to absorb the marvelous flavors and fresh vegetables to round it all out.

MAKE IN ADVANCE

1 batch Fragrant Mixed Mushroom Broth
(page 33)

1 batch Tangy or Savory Soy Dipping
Sauce (page 50)

1 batch Aromatic Scallion and Ginger Oil
(page 51)

HOT-POT INGREDIENTS

1 (10.5-ounce) package or can seitan,
drained if canned

1 (12-ounce) lotus root, peeled and cut into
½-inch rounds

8 ounces oyster mushrooms, halved
if large

8 ounces king oyster mushrooms, cut
lengthwise into ½-inch slices

2 cups straw mushrooms, drained and
rinsed if canned

2 cups button mushrooms, halved

½ medium head broccoli or cauliflower, cut
into 2-inch florets

8 bok choy, outer large leaves halved,
center quartered lengthwise

1 cup bamboo shoot slices, drained
and rinsed

4 bundles mung bean noodles

1. In a 4-quart hot pot, bring the broth to a rolling boil.

2. Let guests cook their own ingredients until tender and cooked through. Cook seitan for 1 to 2 minutes and lotus root slices, mushrooms, broccoli, bok choy, bamboo shoots, and noodles (loosen with a chopstick in the broth) for 1 minute. Adjust the heat to maintain a medium simmer at all times.

3. Serve with the dipping sauce and a dollop of scallion-ginger oil.

4. Replenish the broth as needed as you continue to cook and eat.

VARIATION: Choose your favorite assortment of fresh or dried mushrooms to enjoy.

Add a small dollop of Lao Gan Ma's Chili Crisp, soy sauce, or suggested dipping sauces to enliven foods.

SPICY *MA LA* MIXED VEGETABLE HOT POT

CHINESE, MEATLESS, SPICY

SERVES 4 | PREP TIME: 3 hours 15 minutes (includes soaking) | COOK TIME: 15 minutes

The *ma la* or *ma lat* flavor combining Sichuan chiles and peppercorns produces an appetite-inducing broth for dumplings and vegetables. Cool the spicy sensation lingering on your palate by swishing ingredients in my creamy sesame dip before eating. A bowl of hearty udon noodles holds up to this bold broth for a satisfying finish to your meal.

MAKE IN ADVANCE

1 batch Spicy and Tingly *Ma La* Broth (page 35)

24 Bok Choy, Shiitake, and Chive Dumplings (page 60)

1 batch Creamy Sesame Dipping Sauce (page 53)

HOT-POT INGREDIENTS

1 (5-ounce) package dried bean curd (sold in long strips), broken into 3-inch pieces and soaked in water to cover for 3 hours

1 (4.9-ounce) package fried tofu puffs

2 (3.5-ounce) packages shimeji mushrooms, trimmed and separated into small bundles

1 cup bamboo shoot slices, drained and rinsed

4 celery stalks, peeled and sliced on an angle into ½-inch pieces

¼ head small napa cabbage, cored and cut into 2-inch pieces

8 green leaf lettuce leaves, cut into 3-inch pieces

5 (8.8-ounce) packages frozen udon or thick wheat noodles, cooked al dente and drained

1. In a 4-quart hot pot, bring the broth to a rolling boil.

2. Let guests cook their own ingredients until tender and cooked through. Cook dumplings for about 4 minutes for frozen and 3 minutes for fresh (they are ready when they float to the surface); hydrated bean curd pieces for 2 minutes; tofu puffs, shimeji mushrooms, bamboo shoots, celery, and napa cabbage for 1 to 2 minutes until tender; and lettuce for 30 seconds. Adjust the heat to maintain a medium simmer at all times.

3. Serve with the dipping sauce.

4. Replenish the broth as needed as you continue to cook and eat.

5. Serve udon noodles in a bit of broth to finish the meal.

PAIRING TIP: Counter the spiciness with a tall glass of icy iced tea. For a popular drink pairing with Chinese hot pot, look for Wong Lo Kat or Jia Duo Bao herbal teas sold in bright red cans in the beverage section of Asian supermarkets. Herbal tea is a sweet, noncaffeinated drink made with traditional medicinal ingredients dating from the Qing dynasty. It brings down the body's internal heat and refreshes, especially during a spicy meal.

KIMCHI AND TOFU *CHIGAE* HOT POT

45 MINUTES OR LESS, KOREAN, MEATLESS, SPICY
SERVES 4 | PREP TIME: 15 minutes | COOK TIME: 15 minutes

Kimchi is a staple of Korean cuisine. It is a fermented superfood that is rich in vitamins A and B and minerals like calcium and iron, as well as immune-boosting and high in antioxidants with gut-healthy bacteria. The most common type is napa cabbage with salted shrimp or fish sauce, which aid in fermentation. Nowadays there are more vegan options in the market. Some Korean food companies also make vegan versions. Healthy and delicious, it imparts tangy and spicy flavors in this traditional Korean soybean stew (*chigae*) base with tofu and vegetables.

MAKE IN ADVANCE

1 batch Soybean Broth (page 39)

1 batch Savory Soy Dipping Sauce (page 50)

HOT-POT INGREDIENTS

2 (10.6-ounce) jars mat kimchi (vegetarian or vegan)

1 (16-ounce) package soft tofu or medium tofu, drained and cut into 1-inch cubes

1 (10-ounce) package deep-fried tofu pieces

1 (4.9-ounce) package fried tofu puffs

8 bok choy, outer large leaves halved, center quartered lengthwise

2 medium zucchini, cut into ½-inch slices

8 leaves green leafy lettuce, cut into 3-inch pieces

1 (7-ounce) package enoki mushrooms, trimmed and separated into small bundles

3 cups bean sprouts

Fresh red or green chile peppers, thinly sliced on an angle, for garnish

1. In a 4-quart hot pot, bring the broth to a rolling boil. Stir in the kimchi and its juices. Return to a boil and lower the heat to medium.

2. Let guests cook their own ingredients until tender and cooked through. Cook the assorted tofu, bok choy, and zucchini for 1 to 2 minutes, until tender and cooked through. Cook lettuce, enoki mushrooms, and bean sprouts for 30 seconds.

3. Top with chile peppers. Adjust the heat to maintain a medium simmer at all times.

4. Serve with the dipping sauce.

5. Replenish the broth as needed as you continue to cook and eat.

VARIATION: Combine soft, medium, or firm tofu for a variety of textures.

SPICY RICE CAKE AND DUMPLING HOT POT

45 MINUTES OR LESS, KOREAN, MEATLESS, SPICY
SERVES 4 | PREP TIME: 15 minutes | COOK TIME: 15 minutes

Spicy rice cakes called *tteokbokki* are a popular street food in Korea. As the cylindrical rice cakes simmer in a spicy sauce, they soften and become addictively chewy. The key ingredient is gochujang—a fermented chile paste made with sticky rice paste. Look for it in Asian supermarkets in a red tub. Paired with dumplings, this is a hearty and delicious hot pot rounded out with assorted vegetables. Omit the gochujang for a non-spicy version.

MAKE IN ADVANCE

1 batch Soybean Broth (page 39)

24 Bok Choy, Shiitake, and Chive Dumplings (page 60)

1 batch Tangy Soy Dipping Sauce (page 50)

HOT-POT INGREDIENTS

¼ cup to ½ cup gochujang paste (optional)

1 (10.5-ounce) package rice cakes, thawed if frozen and separated into individual pieces

2 medium carrots, peeled and sliced on an angle into ½-inch pieces

2 leeks, white parts only, sliced on an angle into ½-inch pieces

2 bundles watercress, loosened and halved if pieces are large

¼ head small napa cabbage, cored and cut into 2-inch pieces

2 (3.5-ounce) packages shimeji mushrooms, trimmed and separated into small bundles

3 cups spinach

1. In a 4-quart hot pot, bring the broth to a rolling boil. Stir in the gochujang paste (if using) and cook until dissolved; lower the heat to medium.

2. Let guests cook their own ingredients until tender and cooked through. Cook rice cakes for 5 to 7 minutes or until plump and soft; dumplings for about 4 minutes for frozen and 3 minutes for fresh (they are ready when they float to the surface); carrots and leeks for 2 minutes; and watercress, napa cabbage, and mushrooms for 1 to 2 minutes until tender and cooked through. Cook spinach for 30 seconds. Adjust the heat to maintain a medium simmer at all times.

3. Serve with the dipping sauce.

4. Replenish the broth as needed as you continue to cook and eat.

SUBSTITUTION: Rice cakes are sold fresh and frozen, shaped in cylinders or flat ovals. Instead of rice cakes, use instant or fresh/frozen ramen noodles cooked according to package instructions. If you combine ramen and *tteokbokki*, you will create the popular Korean twist *rabokki*!

TOFU MISO HOT POT

45 MINUTES OR LESS, JAPANESE, MEATLESS
SERVES 4 | PREP TIME: 15 minutes | COOK TIME: 15 minutes

Soothing miso soup is a starter to a Japanese meal, but is used here as a hot-pot broth that lends its mellow tasty comfort throughout the meal. A lighter-fare hot pot, this assortment of tofu, mushrooms, and vegetables is used in numerous varieties and combinations to make miso soup. Healthy buckwheat soba noodles are the perfect light finish.

MAKE IN ADVANCE

1 batch Miso Broth (omit the garlic) (page 39)

1 batch Piquant Soy Dipping Sauce (page 50)

HOT-POT INGREDIENTS

1 (14-ounce) package soba noodles

1 (10-ounce) daikon, peeled and cut into ½-inch moons

1 (16-ounce) package soft or medium tofu, drained and cut into 1-inch cubes

1 (4.9-ounce) package fried tofu puffs

1 cup bamboo shoot slices, drained and rinsed

¼ cup dried cut wakame seaweed

4 cups spinach

1 (7-ounce) package enoki mushrooms, trimmed and separated into small bundles

Nori shreds, for garnish

Scallions, sliced, both white and green parts, for garnish

1. Cook the soba noodles until al dente according to package instructions. Swirl the noodles with chopsticks to separate them. Remove from the heat, transfer to a colander, and rinse thoroughly in running cold water to remove excess starch. Drain well.

2. In a 4-quart hot pot, bring the broth to a rolling boil.

3. Let guests cook their own ingredients until tender and cooked through. Cook daikon for 2 minutes; tofu, fried tofu, and bamboo shoots for 1 to 2 minutes; seaweed for 1 minute; and spinach and mushrooms for 30 seconds. Cooked soba noodles just need to be warmed through. Adjust the heat to maintain a medium simmer at all times.

4. Serve with the dipping sauce. Add nori shreds and scallions to accent tofu and noodles.

5. Replenish the broth as needed as you continue to cook and eat.

VEGETABLE SUKIYAKI

45 MINUTES OR LESS, JAPANESE, MEATLESS
SERVES 4 | PREP TIME: 15 minutes | COOK TIME: 15 minutes

It's all about that stimulating sweet and savory sauce! Start off by sautéing onions and leeks until aromatic. Using cooking chopsticks, cook the vegetables in the caramelizing sauce that adds a sweet glaze, making every bite enjoyable! It's so flavorful, no dipping sauce is required. Tofu and *konnyaku* add heartiness and round out the fresh produce hot pot. Steamed rice often accompanies sukiyaki and is great served on the side.

MAKE IN ADVANCE

1 batch Simple Sukiyaki Sauce (page 56)

HOT-POT INGREDIENTS

2 tablespoons neutral cooking oil, divided

1 large onion, cut into ¼-inch slices

2 leeks, white parts only, sliced on an angle into ½-inch pieces

2 bundles watercress, loosened and halved if pieces are large

1 (16-ounce) package medium or firm tofu, drained and cut into 1-inch cubes

1 cup bamboo shoot slices, drained and rinsed

2 cups *konnyaku*, cut into ½-inch pieces, or bundles, drained and rinsed

½ small (1 pound) kabocha squash, peeled, cut into ¾-inch segments, then halved

¼ head small napa cabbage, cored and cut into 2-inch pieces

8 ounces king oyster mushrooms, cut lengthwise into ½-inch slices

1 (3.5-ounce) package shimeji mushrooms, trimmed and separated into small bundles

Ground cayenne pepper, for garnish

Sesame seeds, for garnish

1. In a 4-quart hot pot or large frying pan, heat 1 tablespoon of oil over medium-high heat. Add the onions and leeks and stir-fry 2 minutes until soft. Move them to one side of the pan.

2. Add ½ cup of sukiyaki sauce. When it comes to a boil, lower the heat to medium.

3. Let guests cook their own ingredients until tender and cooked through. Cook watercress for 2 minutes and tofu, bamboo shoots, *konnyaku*, kabocha squash, napa cabbage, and mushrooms for 1 to 2 minutes. Adjust the heat to maintain a medium simmer at all times.

4. Sprinkle cayenne and sesame seeds on top before eating.

5. Replenish the sauce as needed as you continue to cook and eat. Serve with steamed rice (if using).

HEARTY ROOT VEGETABLE HOT POT

45 MINUTES OR LESS, MEATLESS, VIETNAMESE
SERVES 4 | PREP TIME: 15 minutes | COOK TIME: 15 minutes

Vegetables get a tangy and sweet treatment in this irresistible appetite-whetting broth. Meant to cook and flavor foods, not to serve as a drinking soup, it gets additional layers of tastes with any of the suggested dipping sauces. If you can get fresh sweet pineapples, they will add flavor to the broth as well as absorb its tartness, making it an ideal ingredient to enjoy in this unique hot pot.

MAKE IN ADVANCE

1 batch Tangy and Sweet Broth (*Bò Nhúng Dấm*) (page 43)

1 batch Savory or Piquant Soy Dipping Sauce (page 50)

1 batch Sweet and Sour Chile Sauce (page 54)

INGREDIENTS

1 (6-ounce) daikon, peeled, halved lengthwise, and cut into ½-inch slices

8 ounces king oyster mushrooms, sliced ½-inch lengthwise

1 (10.5-ounce) package or can seitan, drained if canned

1 (1-pound) kabocha squash, peeled, cut into ¾-inch segments, then halved

1 (12-ounce) lotus root, peeled and cut into ½-inch rounds

2 medium carrots, peeled and sliced on an angle into ½-inch pieces

½ medium broccoli or cauliflower, cut into 2-inch florets

1 cup bamboo shoot slices, drained and rinsed

2 cups fresh or canned pineapple chunks

Steamed jasmine rice, for serving

1. In a 4-quart hot pot, bring 10 to 12 cups of broth to a rolling boil.

2. Let guests cook their own ingredients until tender and cooked through. Cook daikon for 2 minutes; mushrooms, seitan, and squash for 1 to 2 minutes; lotus root slices, carrots, broccoli, and bamboo shoots for 1 minute; and pineapple chunks for 30 seconds. Adjust the heat to maintain a medium simmer at all times.

3. Serve with the dipping sauce and eat alongside rice.

4. Replenish the broth as needed as you continue to cook and eat.

SUBSTITUTION: Replace the kabocha with 2 peeled and sliced sweet potatoes.

TOM YUM VEGETABLE HOT POT

GLUTEN-FREE, MEATLESS, THAI
SERVES 4 | PREP TIME: 3 hours 15 minutes (includes soaking) | COOK TIME: 15 minutes

The flavor of tom yum is delightfully lively and comforting at the same time. The aromatics and spicy tanginess enliven vegetables, and the broth gets more flavorful as you cook. The sesame dip gives a layer of nutty creaminess to food while the sweet-and-sour dip extends these flavor notes with a glazed texture. Make sure to enjoy some with rice noodles to complete the meal. Choose your own taste adventure!

MAKE IN ADVANCE

1 batch Hot-and-Sour Tom Yum Broth
(page 46)

1 batch Creamy Sesame Dipping Sauce
(page 53) or Sweet and Sour Chile
Sauce (page 54)

HOT-POT INGREDIENTS

4 medium tomatoes, cut into 8 wedges

1 (5-ounce) package dried bean curd (sold
in long strips), broken into 3-inch pieces
and soaked in water to cover for 3 hours

2 (10.5-ounce) packages or cans seitan,
drained if canned

1½ cups bamboo shoot slices, drained
and rinsed

1 pound oyster mushrooms, chopped
if large

2 cups straw mushrooms, drained and
rinsed if canned, or button mushrooms

8 bok choy, outer large leaves halved,
center quartered lengthwise

1 (1-pound) package rice noodles, cooked
according to package instructions
and drained

Handful Thai basil leaves

1. In a 4-quart hot pot, bring the broth to a rolling boil.

2. Let guests cook their own ingredients until tender and cooked through. Cook tomatoes and hydrated bean curd pieces for 2 minutes, and seitan, bamboo shoot slices, mushrooms, and bok choy for 1 to 2 minutes. Adjust the heat to maintain a medium simmer at all times. Noodles just need to be warmed through.

3. Serve with the dipping sauce. Enjoy with some broth and basil.

4. Replenish the broth as needed as you continue to cook and eat.

SICHUAN *MA LA* FISH HOT POT, PAGE 110

CHAPTER SIX

Meat and Seafood Hot Pots

"EVERYTHING-IN-ONE" HOT POT

45 MINUTES OR LESS, CHICKEN, CHINESE, SEAFOOD
SERVES 4 | PREP TIME: 15 minutes | COOK TIME: 15 minutes

This is my go-to style for hot pot that uses whatever my family or I feel like eating at that moment, and it's a great way to use up any leftover vegetables in my fridge. We like to have a balanced mix of assorted favorite proteins and flavors, including seafood, produce, mushrooms, and dumplings. Our tradition to finish the meal is always with a bowl of fresh rice noodles in the rich and developed broth, slurping and sipping to our hearts' content.

MAKE IN ADVANCE

1 batch All-Purpose Simple Chicken Broth (page 32)

12 Pork and Shrimp Wontons (page 58) or wontons of choice

1 batch Tangy Soy Dipping Sauce (page 50)

HOT-POT INGREDIENTS

1½ pounds boneless chicken thighs or breasts, cut into 1-inch pieces

1 pound large shrimp

1 (16-ounce) package soft or medium tofu, drained and cut into 1-inch cubes

1 (4.9-ounce) package fried tofu puffs

2 cups konnyaku, cut into ½-inch pieces, or bundles, drained and rinsed

2 bundles watercress, loosened and halved if pieces are large

¼ head small napa cabbage, cored and cut into 2-inch pieces

1 (7-ounce) package enoki mushrooms, trimmed and separated into small bundles

1 pound fresh or dried rice noodles, blanched if fresh and cooked according to package instructions if dried, and drained

1. In a 4-quart hot pot, bring the broth to a rolling boil.

2. Let guests cook their own ingredients until tender and cooked through. Cook wontons for about 5 minutes for frozen and 3 minutes for fresh (they are ready when they float to the surface). Cook chicken and shrimp for 2 minutes or until cooked through; tofu, tofu puffs, *konnyaku*, watercress, and napa cabbage for 1 to 2 minutes; and mushrooms for 30 seconds. Adjust the heat to maintain a medium simmer at all times.

3. Serve with the dipping sauce. Noodles just need to be warmed through and enjoyed with the broth.

4. Replenish the broth as needed as you continue to cook and eat.

SUBSTITUTION: Combine your favorites from every category and try something new! I love fish balls in this, too. These would work great in Pork Bone Broth (page 34) or Spicy and Tingly *Ma La* Broth (page 35). Hot-pot broth and ingredients are so versatile that way!

CHANKO NABE SUMO WRESTLER HOT POT

CHICKEN, JAPANESE

SERVES 4 | PREP TIME: 4 hours and 15 minutes (for soaking) | COOK TIME: 15 minutes

What do sumo wrestlers eat to get so strong and hardy? It's a daily diet of chicken and tofu for the main part and lots of vegetables cooked in a *nabe* stew. Delicious and nutritious, it is the food that gives them sustained energy throughout the day. In the morning, they start with vigorous training, then a large bowl of *nabe* for lunch and a snooze. If this can promote endurance and energy for sumos, imagine what it can do for you!

MAKE IN ADVANCE

1 batch All-Purpose Simple Chicken Broth (page 32)

1 batch Homemade Meatballs (Chicken) (page 64)

1 batch Savory Soy Dipping Sauce (page 50)

1 batch Aromatic Scallion and Ginger Oil (page 51)

HOT-POT INGREDIENTS

1½ pounds chicken wings, separated at the joints (tips removed if desired)

12 fresh or dried shiitake mushrooms, soaked in water to cover for 4 hours, stemmed

1 (16-ounce) package medium or firm tofu, drained and cut into 1-inch cubes

8 ounces king oyster mushrooms, cut lengthwise into ½-inch slices

¼ head small napa cabbage, cored and cut into 2-inch pieces

2 cups *konnyaku*, cut into ½-inch pieces, or bundles, drained and rinsed

2 leeks, white parts only, sliced on an angle into ½-inch pieces

5 (8.8-ounce) packages frozen udon or thick wheat noodles, cooked al dente and drained

4 large eggs

1. In a 4-quart hot pot, bring the broth to a rolling boil.

2. Let guests cook their own ingredients until tender and cooked through. Cook meatballs for about 3 minutes for fresh and 5 minutes for frozen (they are ready when they float to the surface); chicken wings for 3 minutes; shiitake mushrooms for 2 minutes; tofu for 1 to 2 minutes; and king oyster mushrooms, napa cabbage, *konnyaku*, and leeks for 1 minute. Adjust the heat to maintain a medium simmer at all times.

3. Serve with dipping sauce with a dollop of scallion and ginger oil.

4. Replenish the broth as needed as you continue to cook and eat.

5. Crack the eggs into the hot pot. For poached, let them simmer undisturbed for 3 to 5 minutes. Serve with broth and udon noodles to finish the meal.

INGREDIENT TIP: Freeze the chicken wing tips in a container to make chicken stock later.

PREP TIP: For a nice presentation, bevel two cross incisions in an "X" on the center tops of whole shiitake mushrooms by inserting the knife diagonally into them and removing the slivers.

MALAYSIAN CURRY *LAKSA* CHICKEN HOT POT

45 MINUTES OR LESS, CHICKEN, GLUTEN-FREE, MALAYSIAN
SERVES 4 | PREP TIME: 15 minutes | COOK TIME: 15 minutes

Laksa is a tasty street noodle soup prepared with curry and coconut milk popular in Malaysia and Singapore. Heartiness and comfort come together with tender chicken, eggs, and an array of complementary vegetables in the rich aromatic broth. Look for the curry paste in an Asian supermarket.

MAKE IN ADVANCE

1 batch Creamy Coconut Broth (page 47)

1 batch Savory or Tangy Soy Dipping Sauce (page 50)

HOT-POT INGREDIENTS

4 lemongrass stalks, white part only, pounded

¼ cup prepared Malaysian/*laksa* curry paste or Thai red curry paste

1½ pounds boneless chicken thighs or breasts, cut into 1-inch pieces

1 (4.9-ounce) package fried tofu puffs

½ medium broccoli or cauliflower, cut into 2-inch florets

8 bok choy, outer large leaves halved, center quartered lengthwise

2 cups straw mushrooms, drained and rinsed if using canned, or button mushrooms

12 quail eggs or 4 large eggs, boiled and peeled

4 cups bean sprouts

1 (10.5-ounce) package vermicelli, cooked according to package instructions and drained

Lime wedges, for garnish

Chopped cilantro, for garnish

1. In a 4-quart hot pot, bring the broth to a rolling boil and add the lemongrass and curry paste. Stir to dissolve and cook for 10 minutes.

2. Let guests cook their own ingredients until tender and cooked through. Cook chicken for 2 minutes; fried tofu, broccoli, bok choy, and straw mushrooms for 1 to 2 minutes; and quail eggs and bean sprouts for 30 seconds. Adjust the heat to maintain a medium simmer at all times.

3. Noodles just need to be warmed through and enjoyed with the broth. Splash with lime juice and add cilantro. Serve with the dipping sauce.

4. Replenish the broth as needed as you continue to cook and eat.

SUBSTITUTION: Instead of chicken, add shrimp and fried fish cakes for a seafood *laksa*.

LAOTIAN PORK SUKIYAKI

45 MINUTES OR LESS, LAOTIAN, PORK
SERVES 4 | PREP TIME: 15 minutes | COOK TIME: 15 minutes

It may share the same name as Japanese sukiyaki, but Laotian sukiyaki is really more like shabu-shabu: cooking in broth you can then drink. Here, it's all about the dipping sauce. Traditionally prepared by cooking shallots, chiles, garlic, and dried shrimp mixed with fermented bean curd and peanuts, I've got an easier version. I combine robust *shacha* barbecue sauce that contains most of these ingredients with peanut butter for creaminess and peanuts for crunch. It tastes incredibly delicious without the extra effort!

MAKE IN ADVANCE

1 batch Pork Bone Broth (page 34) or All-Purpose Simple Chicken Broth (page 32)

1 batch Homemade Meatballs (Pork) (page 64)

12 Meat and Vegetable Dumplings (Pork) (page 62)

HOT-POT INGREDIENTS

1 (16-ounce) package soft or medium tofu, drained and cut into 1-inch cubes

1 (3.5-ounce) package shimeji mushrooms, trimmed and separated into small bundles

4 bundles mung bean noodles

4 celery stalks, peeled and sliced on an angle into ½-inch pieces

1 pound thinly sliced pork (shoulder, butt, jowl, or belly)

4 cups spinach

½ cup *shacha* or *sa cha* barbecue sauce (Bullhead brand or Vegetarian label)

¼ cup crunchy peanut butter (or smooth peanut butter with chopped roasted peanuts)

1. In a 4-quart hot pot, bring the broth to a rolling boil.

2. Let guests cook their own ingredients until tender and cooked through. Cook meatballs and dumplings for about 5 minutes for frozen and 3 minutes for fresh (they are ready when they float to the surface); tofu, mushrooms, and noodles for 1 to 2 minutes; celery for 1 minute; and pork and spinach for 30 seconds. Adjust the heat to maintain a medium simmer at all times.

3. Serve with the dipping sauce: Mix the oil and paste of the *shacha* sauce. In a small bowl, mix the *shacha* sauce and peanut butter, thinned out with water, a teaspoon at a time for consistency.

4. Replenish the broth as needed as you continue to cook and eat.

VARIATION: It is also customary to crack an egg or two directly into the hot pot just before serving, cooking for 1 to 2 minutes.

THAI COCONUT CURRY PORK HOT POT

45 MINUTES OR LESS, PORK, THAI
SERVES 4 | PREP TIME: 15 minutes | COOK TIME: 15 minutes

Creamy coconut curry dishes are popular in Thai cuisine and pack some heat. Home-style versions are conveniently made with store-bought concentrated curry paste with green being the most spicy, then medium red and milder yellow, which tends to be sweet. Added to give more depth to tom yum broth, the coconut milk counters the spiciness, making it lovely for hot-pot ingredients.

MAKE IN ADVANCE

10 cups Hot-and-Sour Tom Yum Broth (page 46)

12 Meat and Vegetable Dumplings (Pork) (page 62) or store-bought pork dumplings

1 batch Savory Soy Dipping Sauce (page 50)

HOT-POT INGREDIENTS

4 (13.5-ounce) cans full-fat coconut milk

¼ cup prepared Thai red curry paste

8 ounces mussels on the half shell or squid (optional)

1 (1-pound) kabocha squash, peeled, cut into ¾-inch segments, then halved

1 (16-ounce) package soft or medium tofu, drained and cut into 1-inch cubes

1 (4.9-ounce) package fried tofu puffs

8 ounces king oyster mushrooms, cut lengthwise into ½-inch slices

1½ cups bamboo shoot slices, drained and rinsed

1½ pounds thinly sliced pork (shoulder, butt, jowl, or belly)

3 cups bean sprouts

Thai basil leaves

1. In a 4-quart hot pot, bring 3 cans of coconut milk to a boil over medium-high heat.

2. Lower the heat to medium and add the red curry paste; stir to dissolve, cooking for 1 to 2 minutes until the oil of the coconut milk rises to the surface. Carefully add 9 cups of the broth and bring back to a rolling boil.

3. Let guests cook their own ingredients until tender and cooked through. Cook the dumplings for about 5 minutes for frozen and 3 minutes for fresh (they are ready when they float to the surface); the mussels and kabocha squash for 2 minutes; tofu and fried tofu for 1 to 2 minutes; king mushrooms and bamboo shoots for 1 minute; and pork slices and bean sprouts for 30 seconds. Adjust the heat to maintain a medium simmer at all times.

4. Noodles just need to be warmed through. Enjoy with some broth and basil. Serve with the dipping sauce.

5. Replenish the broth as needed with the remaining 1 cup of broth and can of coconut milk as you continue to cook and eat. If you need more broth, a kettle of boiling hot water will work.

KOREAN SPICY ARMY STEW HOT POT

45 MINUTES OR LESS, KOREAN, PORK, SPICY
SERVES 4 | PREP TIME: 15 minutes | COOK TIME: 15 minutes

Korean army stew or army base stew (*budae jjigae*) is one of the most popular hot-pot styles in Korea. It uses some out-of-the-ordinary ingredients such as Spam, hot dogs, and processed cheese. Interesting fact: soon after the Korean war (in the early 1950s), food was extremely scarce, so surplus processed foods from the US military bases were a great supplement for the Koreans, thus the creation of a Korean-American fusion stew. Savory, spicy, and delicious, the melted cheese gives the stew a slightly creamy dimension.

MAKE IN ADVANCE

1 batch Pork Bone Broth (page 34) or All-Purpose Simple Chicken Broth (page 32)

1 batch Tangy Soy Dipping Sauce (page 50)

HOT-POT INGREDIENTS

1 to 2 (10.6-ounce) jars mat kimchi

3 to 4 (3-ounce) packs of spicy instant ramen noodles (and the spicy seasoning packets)

2 (12-ounce) cans Spam, cut into bite-size pieces

8 hot dogs, cut into bite-size pieces

1 (16-ounce) package soft or medium tofu, drained and cut into 1-inch cubes

2 medium zucchini, cut into ½-inch slices

8 ounces oyster mushrooms, chopped if large

1 (7-ounce) package enoki mushrooms, trimmed and separated into small bundles

4 slices processed cheese (such as Kraft American Singles)

Sliced scallions, both white and green parts, for garnish

1. In a 4-quart hot pot, bring the broth to a rolling boil. Stir in the kimchi and its juices. Add 1 spicy seasoning packet. Stir, taste, and adjust the seasoning to your preferred spice level.

2. Let guests cook their own ingredients until tender and cooked through. Cook ramen noodles for 2 minutes; Spam and hot dogs for 1 to 2 minutes until tender and cooked through; tofu, zucchini, and oyster mushrooms for 1 minute; and enoki mushrooms for 30 seconds. Lay the cheese on top of the broth for 10 seconds and ladle into bowls to serve. Adjust the heat to maintain a medium simmer at all times.

3. Serve with the dipping sauce and scallions.

4. Replenish the broth as needed as you continue to cook and eat.

INGREDIENT TIP: Two top brands of kimchi from Korea that are loaded with flavor are Chongga and Jongga.

SUBSTITUTION: Instead of hot dogs and/or Spam, use 1½ pounds thinly sliced pork (shoulder, butt, jowl, or belly).

TAIWANESE *SHACHA* BARBECUE BEEF SHABU-SHABU

BEEF, SPICY, TAIWANESE

SERVES 4 | PREP TIME: 3 hours and 15 minutes (includes soaking) | COOK TIME: 15 minutes

Ingredients first cook in the robust savory broth, then its irresistible *shacha* flavor doubles as a dipping sauce with beaten egg. The developed simmering flavors are likened to a cookout barbecue but in a hot pot instead of on the grill: smoky, tasty, and incredibly satiating!

MAKE IN ADVANCE

1 batch Easy Smoky *Shacha* Barbecue Broth (page 38)

1 batch Homemade Meatballs (Beef) (page 64) or 1 (16-ounce) package beef balls

1 batch Silky Egg and *Shacha* Barbecue Sauce (page 52)

HOT-POT INGREDIENTS

1 (5-ounce) package dried bean curd (sold in long strips), broken into 3-inch pieces and soaked in water to cover for 3 hours

1 (16-ounce) package medium or firm tofu, drained and cut into 1-inch cubes

8 ounces king oyster mushrooms, cut lengthwise into ½-inch slices

1 cup bamboo shoot slices, drained and rinsed

2 bundles watercress, loosened and halved if pieces are large

8 leaves green leafy lettuce, cut into 3-inch pieces

1½ pounds thinly sliced beef (combination of brisket, sirloin, top blade, or chuck)

1 (10.5-ounce) package vermicelli, cooked according to package instructions and drained

1. In a 4-quart hot pot, bring the broth to a rolling boil.

2. Let guests cook their own ingredients until tender and cooked through. Cook the meatballs for about 4 minutes for frozen and 3 minutes for fresh (they are ready when they float to the surface); hydrated bean curd pieces, tofu, mushrooms, and bamboo shoots for 1 to 2 minutes; watercress for 1 minute; and lettuce greens and beef for 30 seconds. Adjust the heat to maintain a medium simmer at all times.

3. Serve with the dipping sauce. Noodles just need to be warmed through and enjoyed with some broth.

4. Replenish the broth as needed as you continue to cook and eat.

SUBSTITUTION: Replace beef with lamb or combine both for variety.

JAPANESE BEEF SUKIYAKI

45 MINUTES OR LESS, BEEF, JAPANESE
SERVES 4 | PREP TIME: 15 minutes | COOK TIME: 15 minutes

Japanese sukiyaki is all about the full-bodied sweet and savory sauce, as it cooks down into a caramelized glaze along with thin marbled beef slices. The beef fat adds to the delicious taste and tender mouthfeel. My first sukiyaki dinner was in Japan with my brother and sister-in-law nearly two decades ago. They used long chopsticks to swish the meat in the simmering sauce, dipped into a beaten fresh egg before slurping it down. Just beautiful, and so luxurious!

MAKE IN ADVANCE
1 batch Simple Sukiyaki Sauce (page 56)

HOT-POT INGREDIENTS

2 tablespoons neutral cooking oil, divided

1 large onion, cut into ¼-inch slices

2 leeks, white parts only, sliced on an angle into ½-inch pieces

1 (7-ounce) package tofu fish cakes

½ medium broccoli, cut into 2-inch florets

1 (16-ounce) package medium or firm tofu, drained and cut into 1-inch cubes

8 bok choy, outer large leaves halved, center quartered lengthwise

2 cups *konnyaku*, cut into ½-inch pieces, or bundles, drained and rinsed

1 (7-ounce) package enoki mushrooms, trimmed and separated into small bundles

2 pounds thinly sliced beef (combination of brisket, sirloin, top blade, or chuck)

4 large eggs (pasteurized), beaten into 4 individual bowls for dipping

Cayenne pepper or sesame seeds, for garnish

Steamed rice (optional)

1. In a 4-quart hot pot or large frying pan, heat 1 tablespoon of oil to medium-high heat. Add the onions and leeks and stir-fry for 2 minutes until soft. Move them to one side of the pan.

2. Add ½ cup of sukiyaki sauce. When it comes to a boil, bring the heat down to medium.

3. Let guests cook their own ingredients until tender and cooked through. Cook frozen fish cakes for 3 minutes and fresh for 2 minutes; broccoli, tofu, bok choy, and *konnyaku* for 1 to 2 minutes; mushrooms for 1 minute; and beef slices for 30 seconds. Adjust the heat to maintain a medium simmer at all times.

4. Serve with raw egg. Sprinkle cayenne or sesame seeds on top before eating.

5. Replenish the sauce as needed as you continue to cook and eat. Serve with rice (if using).

VARIATION: Instead of serving with raw egg as a dip, break an egg over the beef in the hot pot to cook to your desired doneness.

BÒ NHÚNG DẤM BEEF HOT POT

45 MINUTES OR LESS, BEEF, GLUTEN-FREE, VIETNAMESE
SERVES 4 | PREP TIME: 15 minutes | COOK TIME: 15 minutes

Beef and vegetables get a tangy and sweet treatment in this irresistible appetite-whetting broth. My Vietnamese husband and family-in-law serve *bò nhúng dấm* in a traditional chafing dish cooked at the center of the table. Chopsticks are used to cook instead of ladles. The fun part is wrapping the cooked beef, noodles, accompanying vegetables and herbs in rice paper and into parcels, then dipping in fish sauce. All other hot-pot items are eaten on the side.

MAKE IN ADVANCE

1 batch Tangy and Sweet Broth (*Bò Nhúng Dấm*) (page 43)

1 batch Seasoned Fish Sauce (*Nuoc Mam Cham*) (page 55)

INGREDIENTS

6 ounces squid tubes, cartilage removed and rinsed, or raw calamari rings (optional)

1 (6-ounce) daikon, peeled, halved lengthwise, and cut into ½-inch slices

12 fresh or dried shiitake mushrooms, soaked in water to cover for 4 hours, stemmed and halved if large

1 (12-ounce) lotus root, peeled and cut into ½-inch rounds

¼ head small napa cabbage, cored and cut into 2-inch pieces

3 cups spinach

2 cups fresh or canned pineapple chunks

12 quail eggs, boiled and peeled

2 pounds thinly sliced beef (combination of brisket, sirloin, top blade, or chuck)

1 (10.5-ounce) package vermicelli, cooked according to package instructions and drained

Fresh red or green chile peppers, thinly sliced on an angle for garnish

1. Slice the squid tubes open and score into a diamond pattern. Cut into 1½-inch strips.

2. In a 4-quart hot pot, bring 10 to 12 cups of broth to a rolling boil.

3. Let guests cook their own ingredients until tender and cooked through. Cook daikon and shiitake mushrooms for 2 minutes; lotus root slices and napa cabbage for 1 to 2 minutes; squid for 1 minute; and spinach, pineapples, quail eggs, and beef slices for 30 seconds. Top with chile peppers. Adjust the heat to maintain a medium simmer at all times.

4. Serve with the dipping sauce or prepare the traditional way in the Variation before dipping. Noodles just need to be warmed through and enjoyed with some broth.

5. Replenish the broth as needed as you continue to cook and eat.

VARIATION: To serve these in rice paper, prepare lettuce leaves, vermicelli, sliced cucumbers, bean sprouts, fresh mint, Thai basil, cilantro, and 2-inch pieces of Asian chives. Soak rice paper sheets, one at a time as you use them, in warm water for 5 seconds. Remove and place a piece of leaf lettuce onto the lower half of the wet rice paper. Layer with other ingredients. Fold up the bottom, then the sides and roll up and over to seal. Dip in the seasoned fish sauce.

VIETNAMESE BEEF PHO HOT POT

45 MINUTES OR LESS, BEEF, GLUTEN-FREE, VIETNAMESE
SERVES 4 | PREP TIME: 15 minutes | COOK TIME: 15 minutes

The iconic bowl of Vietnamese pho is hearty and beloved. It dawned on me during my travel in Vietnam how immensely pho was enjoyed, easily at every meal starting from the crack of dawn. A staple fuel normally eaten quickly to go about the day, how about we slow it down and enjoy it in small doses with company and conversations? And thus emerges the laid-back style of pho hot pot!

MAKE IN ADVANCE

1 batch Savory Pho Beef Broth (page 44)

½ batch Homemade Meatballs (Beef) (page 64) or 8-ounces beef balls (with tendon is ideal)

HOT-POT INGREDIENTS

1 pound boneless chicken thighs or breasts, cut into 1-inch pieces (optional)

1 (6-ounce) daikon, peeled, halved lengthwise, and cut into ½-inch slices

1 (4.9-ounce) package fried tofu puffs

8 bok choy, outer large leaves halved, center quartered lengthwise

1½ pounds thinly sliced beef (combination of beef brisket, sirloin, top blade, or chuck)

3 cups bean sprouts

1 pound fresh rice noodles or packaged rice sticks, blanched if fresh and cooked according to package instructions if dried, and drained

Sliced scallions, for garnish

Chopped fresh cilantro, for garnish

1. In a 4-quart hot pot, bring the broth to a rolling boil.

2. Let guests cook their own ingredients until tender and cooked through. Cook meatballs for about 4 minutes for frozen and 3 minutes for fresh (they are ready when they float to the surface); chicken and daikon for 2 minutes; fried tofu and bok choy for 1 to 2 minutes; and beef slices and bean sprouts for 30 seconds. Adjust the heat to maintain a medium simmer at all times.

3. Noodles just need to be warmed through and enjoyed with the broth. Top with scallions and cilantro.

4. Replenish the broth as needed as you continue to cook and eat.

PAIRING TIP: This is popularly served with a mix of hoisin sauce and sriracha hot sauce for dipping.

SPICY MONGOLIAN LAMB HOT POT

45 MINUTES OR LESS, MONGOLIAN, LAMB, SPICY
SERVES 4 | PREP TIME: 15 minutes | COOK TIME: 15 minutes

This traditional full-bodied broth goes well with the stronger taste of lamb in a nod to its Mongol origins. As it can get very spicy, the ideal ingredients are ones that are not absorbent. You will enjoy the ingredients better without needing to extinguish your palate between bites. Follow the broth recipe to create both a spicy and non-spicy version to enjoy in a split pot. Beef instead of lamb tastes delicious in here, too!

MAKE IN ADVANCE

1 batch Spicy and Herbal Lamb Broth
   (page 36)
½ batch Homemade Meatballs (Lamb)
   (page 64) or 1 (8-ounce) or ½ (16-ounce)
   package beef balls
1 batch Creamy Sesame Dipping Sauce
   (page 53)

HOT-POT INGREDIENTS

1 (1-pound) kabocha squash, peeled, cut
   into ¾-inch segments, then halved
1 (16-ounce) package soft or medium tofu,
   drained and cut into 1-inch cubes
8 bok choy, outer large leaves halved,
   center quartered lengthwise
1½ cups bamboo shoot slices, drained
   and rinsed
2 cups straw mushrooms, drained and
   rinsed if canned
½ medium head broccoli, cut into
   2-inch florets
1½ pounds boneless lamb, thinly sliced
1 (1-pound) package thick wheat
   noodles, cooked according to package
   instructions and drained

1. In a 4-quart hot pot, bring the broth to a rolling boil.

2. Let guests cook their own ingredients until tender and cooked through. Cook meatballs for about 4 minutes for frozen and 3 minutes for fresh (they are ready when they float to the surface); squash for 2 minutes; tofu, bok choy, bamboo shoots, straw mushrooms, and broccoli for 1 minute; and lamb for 30 seconds. Adjust the heat to maintain a medium simmer at all times.

3. Serve with the dipping sauce. Noodles just need to be warmed through and enjoyed with the broth.

4. Replenish the broth as needed as you continue to cook and eat.

SUBSTITUTION: Use a prepared hot-pot broth mix such as Little Sheep Hot Pot in non-spicy and/ or spicy flavors.

VARIATION: This recipe is great with king oyster mushrooms added, cut lengthwise into ½-inch slices.

LAMB SHABU-SHABU

45 MINUTES OR LESS, JAPANESE, LAMB, SPICY
SERVES 4 | PREP TIME: 15 minutes | COOK TIME: 15 minutes

In Hokkaido, Japan's mountainous north, paper-thin lamb slices are enjoyed with a mellow broth alongside mushrooms and fresh vegetables dipped in a complementary spicy sauce. Lamb meatballs add a dense and springy texture in lamb shabu-shabu, but they are not found in stores. Try making my homemade recipe on page 64, and prepare the spicy version for a heat kick to perk things up.

MAKE IN ADVANCE

1 batch Dashi Broth (page 40)

1 batch Homemade Meatballs (Lamb) (page 64) or 1 (16-ounce) package beef balls

1 batch Piquant Soy Dipping Sauce (page 50) or Sweet and Sour Chile Sauce (page 54)

HOT-POT INGREDIENTS

12 fresh or dried shiitake mushrooms, soaked in water to cover for 4 hours, stemmed and halved if large

1 (4.9-ounce) package fried tofu puffs

1 pound oyster mushrooms, chopped if large

2 leeks, green parts removed, sliced on an angle into ½-inch pieces

8 leaves green leafy lettuce, cut into 3-inch pieces

4 cups spinach

1½ pounds thinly sliced lamb

1 package fresh or frozen ramen, cooked according to package instructions and drained

1. In a 4-quart hot pot, bring the broth to a rolling boil.

2. Let guests cook their own ingredients until tender and cooked through. Cook meatballs for about 4 minutes for frozen and 3 minutes for fresh (they are ready when they float to the surface); shiitake mushrooms and fried tofu for 2 minutes; oyster mushrooms and leeks for 1 minute; and lettuce, spinach, and lamb for 30 seconds. Adjust the heat to maintain a medium simmer at all times.

3. Serve with the dipping sauce. Noodles just need to be warmed through and enjoyed with the broth.

4. Replenish the broth as needed as you continue to cook and eat.

SUBSTITUTION: Thinly sliced beef or pork can be used instead of lamb.

SICHUAN *MA LA* FISH HOT POT

45 MINUTES OR LESS, CHINESE, SEAFOOD, SPICY
SERVES 4 | PREP TIME: 15 minutes | COOK TIME: 15 minutes

This popular Sichuan casserole dish prepared with delicate, mild-tasting white fish gently poaches until it's moist and tender. The addictive *ma la* flavor is exquisite, and the fish texture is sublime! A swish in vinegar dip is the prime taming counterpoint to the spice-doused ingredients. Add a dollop of scallion and ginger oil that goes oh so well with fish. I personally love adding mung bean noodles to absorb the spicy flavors. Try that instead of wheat noodles if you like it spicy!

MAKE IN ADVANCE

1 batch Spicy and Tingly *Ma La* Broth (page 35)

1 batch Sichuan Spicy *Ma La* Marinated Fish (page 63)

1 batch Tangy Soy Dipping Sauce (page 50)

1 batch Aromatic Scallion and Ginger Oil (page 51)

HOT-POT INGREDIENTS

1 (7-ounce) package tofu fish cakes or fried fish cakes

1 (16-ounce) package soft or medium tofu, drained and cut into 1-inch cubes

2 (3.5-ounce) packages shimeji mushrooms, trimmed and separated into small bundles

1 cup bamboo shoot slices, drained and rinsed

4 celery stalks, peeled and sliced on an angle into ½-inch pieces

¼ small napa cabbage head, cored and cut into 2-inch pieces

8 green leafy lettuce leaves, cut into 3-inch pieces

5 (8.8-ounce) packages frozen udon or thick wheat noodles, cooked al dente and drained

1. In a 4-quart hot pot, bring the broth to a rolling boil.

2. Let guests cook their own ingredients until tender and cooked through. Cook tofu fish cakes for about 3 minutes for frozen and 2 minutes for fresh (they are ready when they float to the surface); tofu, shimeji mushrooms, bamboo shoots, celery, napa cabbage, and fish for 1 to 2 minutes until tender; and lettuce for 30 seconds. Adjust the heat to maintain a medium simmer at all times.

3. Serve with the dipping sauces.

4. Replenish the broth as needed as you continue to cook and eat.

5. Serve udon noodles in a bit of broth to finish the meal.

INGREDIENT TIP: Fish pieces are delicate; it is best to cook them in a ladle basket.

SUBSTITUTION: Instead of noodles, you can use chewy rice cake.

JAPANESE *ODEN* (FISH CAKE STEW) HOT POT

45 MINUTES OR LESS, JAPANESE, SEAFOOD
SERVES 4 | PREP TIME: 15 minutes | COOK TIME: 15 minutes

A classic comfort dish in Japan during winter, *oden* is a one-pot dish of fish balls and tofu. Simmering in a soy sauce and dashi broth is an assortment of fish balls, fish cakes, *konnyaku*, tofu, fried tofu, hard-boiled eggs, and some vegetables. Leftover broth is eagerly enjoyed the next day, as it always tastes better! Also try this with my milky broth for another fish-base alternative.

MAKE IN ADVANCE

10 cups Dashi Broth (page 40) or Milky White Fish Broth (page 42)

1 batch Simple Sukiyaki Sauce (page 56)

1 batch Piquant Soy Dipping Sauce (page 50) or wasabi, hot mustard, or Dijon mustard

HOT-POT INGREDIENTS

2 (18-ounce) packages assorted fish balls, including fried fish cakes

1 (6-ounce) daikon, peeled and cut into ½-inch half-moons

1 (16-ounce) package soft or medium tofu, drained and cut into 1-inch cubes

1 (4.9-ounce) package fried tofu puffs

2 cups *konnyaku*, cut into ½-inch pieces, or bundles, drained and rinsed

¼ cup dried wakame seaweed

1 (8-ounce) package imitation crab sticks, cut into bite-size pieces

2 leeks, white parts only, sliced on an angle into ½-inch pieces

12 quail eggs or 4 eggs, boiled and peeled

Nori shreds and scallions, for garnish

1. In a 4-quart hot pot, bring the broth and sukiyaki sauce to a rolling boil.

2. Let guests cook their own ingredients until tender and cooked through. Cook frozen fish balls for about 4 minutes and 3 minutes for fresh (they are ready when they float to the surface); daikon for 2 minutes; tofu, fried tofu, and *konnyaku* for 1 to 2 minutes; seaweed, crab sticks, and leeks for 1 minute; and the cooked eggs for 30 seconds. Adjust the heat to maintain a medium simmer at all times.

3. Serve with the dipping sauce or just wasabi, hot mustard, or Dijon mustard. Also add nori shreds and scallions to accent tofu and ingredients.

4. Replenish the broth as needed as you continue to cook and eat. A hot water kettle will do.

INGREDIENT TIP: Look for prepared *oden* ingredients in the freezer section of your nearest Japanese market.

VARIATION: For fun, use long wooden skewers to skewer three or four items at a time, fish balls or tofu and leeks, according to same cook times. You can also add bite-size hot dogs. Dip in the hot pot to cook instead of using a ladle.

FILIPINO FISH SINIGANG HOT POT

45 MINUTES OR LESS, FILIPINO, SEAFOOD
SERVES 4 | PREP TIME: 15 minutes | COOK TIME: 15 minutes

Seafood tastes delicious in this popular Filipino soup that enhances your appetite with its sour notes. Dried anchovy (*iriko*) or milky fish is a fantastic starter broth that serves up health-boosting minerals. Together with tangy tamarind, the flavors will develop temptingly with all your hot-pot ingredients. Save any leftover broth for the next day to enjoy again!

MAKE IN ADVANCE

1 batch Iriko Broth (page 41) or Milky White Fish Broth (page 42)

1 batch Savory Soy Dipping Sauce (page 50)

1 batch Aromatic Scallion and Ginger Oil (page 51)

HOT-POT INGREDIENTS

2 (1.4-ounce) packets tamarind soup mix

2 tablespoons granulated sugar

1 large onion, sliced

4 large tomatoes, each cut into 8 wedges

1 (6-ounce) daikon, peeled, halved lengthwise, and cut into ½-inch slices

1 pound shrimp, rinsed and drained

12 bok choy, outer large leaves halved, center quartered lengthwise

1½ cups bamboo shoot slices, drained and rinsed

1½ pounds boneless fish fillets (salmon or white fish), thinly sliced into bite-size pieces

Steamed rice

1. In a 4-quart hot pot, bring the broth to a rolling boil. Dissolve the tamarind soup mix and sugar in it, then add the onion slices.

2. Let guests cook their own ingredients until tender and cooked through. Cook the tomatoes, daikon, and shrimp for 2 minutes until tender, and cook the bok choy, bamboo shoots, and fish for 1 minute. Adjust the heat to maintain a medium simmer at all times.

3. Serve with the dipping sauce with a dollop of scallion and ginger oil.

4. Replenish the broth as needed as you continue to cook and eat.

5. Serve with steamed rice.

VARIATION: To make a whole-fish hot pot, make an all-in-one fish hot-pot broth and choose a fish that fits your hot pot nicely. Scale and gut the fish (or ask your fishmonger to do this), rinse well, remove the fins, place in your hot pot, fill with water to cover, and simmer until fully cooked. Carefully transfer it whole to a plate (to enjoy) before adding other ingredients.

YA-HON CAMBODIAN SEAFOOD HOT POT

45 MINUTES OR LESS, BEEF, CAMBODIAN, SEAFOOD
SERVES 4 | PREP TIME: 15 minutes | COOK TIME: 15 minutes

Creamy coconut complements the brininess of seafood, so choose your favorites for this Cambodian special. The more *shacha* sauce you add, the spicier it will taste, giving a lovely orange slick to the white broth. Both noodles and steamed rice are common to eat with *ya-hon*, so choose whichever you prefer to serve with it.

MAKE IN ADVANCE

1 batch Creamy Coconut Broth (page 47)
1 batch Savory or Tangy Soy Dipping
  Sauce (page 50)

HOT-POT INGREDIENTS

8 ounces fish or seafood balls

2 cups *konnyaku*, cut into ½-inch pieces, or bundles or noodles, drained and rinsed

2 bundles watercress, loosened and cut in half if pieces are large

8 bok choy, outer large leaves halved, center quartered lengthwise

1 (7-ounce) package enoki mushrooms, trimmed and separated into small bundles

12 quail eggs or 4 eggs, boiled and peeled

1 pound salmon fillet, cut into ½-inch bite-size pieces

1 pound thinly sliced beef (combination of brisket, sirloin, top blade, or chuck)

1 (1-pound) package vermicelli or dried rice sticks, cooked according to package instructions and drained

1. In a 4-quart hot pot, bring the broth to a rolling boil.

2. Let guests cook their own ingredients until tender and cooked through. Cook fish balls for about 4 minutes for frozen and 3 minutes for fresh (they are ready when they float to the surface); *konnyaku*, watercress, and bok choy for 1 to 2 minutes; and enoki mushrooms, quail eggs, salmon slices, and beef slices for 30 seconds. Adjust the heat to maintain a medium simmer at all times.

3. Noodles just need to be warmed through, then enjoy with the broth.

4. Serve with the dipping sauce.

5. Replenish the broth as needed as you continue to cook and eat.

SUBSTITUTION: Replace the beef with your choice of seafood. Or, replace the salmon with Sichuan Spicy *Ma La* Marinated Fish (page 63).

THAI SPICY SEAFOOD MEDLEY SUKI

45 MINUTES OR LESS, SEAFOOD, SPICY, THAI
SERVES 4 | PREP TIME: 15 minutes | COOK TIME: 15 minutes

Seafood lovers rejoice in this delectable mixed seafood hot pot with the fragrant, spicy, and sour notes of tom yum. Hot pot in Thailand is known as Thai *suki*, which resembles shabu-shabu-style hot pot more than Japanese sukiyaki (where the name was adopted). The favored dip is a mix of lime, chile sauce, and cilantro, which pairs deliciously with these hearty ingredients. You can also use the Savory Soy Dipping Sauce on page 50.

MAKE IN ADVANCE

1 batch Hot-and-Sour Tom Yum Broth (page 46)

12 Pork and Shrimp Wontons (page 58)

HOT-POT INGREDIENTS

6 ounces squid tubes, cartilage removed and rinsed, or raw calamari rings

16 ounces assorted fish balls

8 ounces mussels on the half shell, rinsed and drained

1 pound large shrimp, rinsed and drained

8 bok choy, outer large leaves halved, center quartered lengthwise

2 cups button mushrooms, halved

2 cups *konnyaku*, cut into ½-inch pieces, or bundles, drained and rinsed

1 (8-ounce) package imitation crab sticks, cut into bite-size pieces

8 bundles mung bean noodles

Sriracha (optional)

Fresh lime juice (optional)

Chopped cilantro (optional)

1. Slice the squid tubes open and score into a diamond pattern. Cut into 1½-inch strips.

2. In a 4-quart hot pot or large saucepan, bring the broth to a boil.

3. Let guests cook their own ingredients until tender and cooked through. Cook wontons and fish balls for about 5 minutes for frozen and 3 minutes for fresh (they are ready when they float to the surface); mussels and shrimp for 2 minutes; and squid, bok choy, mushrooms, *konnyaku*, crab sticks, and noodles (loosen with a chopstick in the broth) for 1 minute.

4. Serve with the dipping sauce or try sriracha hot sauce mixed with lime juice and chopped cilantro.

5. Replenish the broth as needed as you continue to cook and eat.

PAIRING TIP: Tame the heat with a sip of juice from a cold fresh coconut.

VARIATION: Sliced fish fillet pieces are great to add in.

Resources

ONLINE AND IN-STORE GROCERY

Asian Food Grocer (Online Asian Groceries and Products) AsianFoodGrocer.com

E Food Depot (Online Japanese, Indonesian, and Thai Groceries and Products) EFoodDepot.com

99 Ranch (Asian Groceries and Products) 99ranch.com

H Mart (Korean Groceries and Products) HMart.com

Mitsuwa Market (Japanese Groceries and Products) Mitsuwa.com

Seafood City (Filipino Groceries and Products) SeafoodCity.com

TO LEARN MORE ABOUT HOT POT

Aguilar, Michelle. "Hot Pot: From Food to Culture." Medium. August 6, 2018. Medium.com/@michelleaguilar_90524/hot-pot-from-food-to-culture-ebd2eb050054.

Chen, Karissa. "It's Always Hot Pot Season in Taipei." Eater. March 6, 2019. eater.com/2019/3/6/18242556/hot-pot-how-to-eat-taipei-tips.

Chen, Vincent. *Hot Pot Night!* Watertown, MA: Charlesbridge Publishing, 2020.

Life of Guangzhou. "The History of Hot Pot in China." March 5, 2021. Lifeofguangzhou.com/knowGZ/content.do?contextId=13159&frontParentCatalogId=175.

Zhang, Tingwei. "Chinese Hotpot: A Communal Food Culture." December 22, 2019. Storymaps.arcgis.com/stories/9c3a733c1411400e9f80310fa8b65a9e.

References

Chen, Namiko. "Konnyaku (Konjac)." *Just One Cookbook* (blog). Last modified January 22, 2021. Justonecookbook.com/konjac-konnyaku.

Foshan Wanyene Furniture. "How the Hot Pot History and the Origin of Hot Pot Influence People's Lives." September 3, 2018. Hotpotset.com/article-184.html.

Goldthread. "The Best Hidden Restaurants in Chongqing." December 13, 2019. Today.line.me/hk/v2/article/r2NEZw.

Hongyu, Bianji. "Hotpot, Barbecue Can Be Traced Back to China's Han Dynasty." People's Daily Online. May 25, 2016. En.people.cn/n3/2016/0525/c98649-9063044.html.

McDermott, Anna. "The Nutritional Value of Soba Noodles." Healthline. Last modified October 12, 2017. Healthline.com/health/food-nutrition/soba-noodles-nutrition#Soba-Noodle-Nutrition.

Index

ACKNOWLEDGMENTS

I'd like to thank my boisterous family: my husband, Quoc, for his support and for entertaining the kids while I plugged away at writing, and my boys—Étienne, Sébastien, and Matias—for the boundless fun and for enduring the summer heat eating hot pot during the recipe development phase. Thank goodness for AC! My mother, for nurturing my love for cooking. My father, for instilling in me that *knowledge is power* and cross-checking my hot-pot references against Chinese literature. My brother, Marten Go, and sister-in-law, Yoko, for introducing me to hot pots in Japan and for their recipe feedback. My sister, Trai, for believing I could do this amid my busy teaching schedule. A special thank-you to my best friend, Huong, for encouraging me from the very beginning and being my cheerleader as I worked through every milestone. My niece, Kathia, work partners, and students for their enthusiasm and support with my exciting book announcement. And the incredible team at Rockridge Press for their guidance and getting me through seamlessly to the finish line. The inspiration I got from all of you kept me keeping on. Having my own cookbook is a dream come true!

ABOUT THE AUTHOR

Susan Ng is a culinary consultant and food educator. Her passion is to inspire people of all ages to get in the kitchen to cook, eat healthy, and learn about multiculturalism by trying different cuisines. She instructs cooking classes and designs culinary programs through school and community collaborations. She lives in Toronto, Ontario, Canada, with her husband and three children. You can find her sharing new food adventures at work and play @susanssavourit and susanssavourit.blogspot.ca.

CPSIA information can be obtained
at www.ICGtesting.com
Printed in the USA
JSHW040705261221
21521JS00003B/4

9 781638 070238